20 Good Reasons
to Study the Civil War

Books by John C. Waugh

The Class of 1846: From West Point to Appomattox—Stonewall Jackson, George McClellan and Their Brothers

Reelecting Lincoln: The Battle for the 1864 Presidency

Surviving the Confederacy: Rebellion, Ruin, and Recovery—Roger and Sara Pryor During the Civil War

On the Brink of Civil War: The Compromise of 1850 and How It Changed the Course of American History

Sam Bell Maxey and the Confederate Indians

Last Stand at Mobile

Edwin Cole Bearss: History's Pied Piper

20 Good Reasons
to Study the Civil War

John C. Waugh

McWhiney Foundation Press
McMurry University
Abilene, Texas

Library of Congress Cataloging-in-Publication Data

Waugh, John C.
    20 good reasons to study the Civil War / John C. Waugh.
      p. cm.
    ISBN 1-893114-46-5 (pbk. : alk. paper)
    1. United States--History--Civil War, 1861-1865--Study
and teaching. 2. United States--History--Civil War, 1861-1865--
Miscellanea. 3. United States--History--Civil War, 1861-1865--
Influence. I. Title: Twenty good reasons to study the Civil War.
II. Title.
      E468.5.W38 2004
      973.7'071--dc22

                                2004001876

McWhiney Foundation Press
McMurry Station, Box 637
Abilene, TX 79697-0637
(325) 793-4682
www.mcwhiney.org

Printed in the United States of America

1-893114-46-5 paper
10 9 8 7 6 5 4 3 2 1

Book designed by Rosenbohm Graphic Design

Contents

For Edwin Cole Bearss, who knows all the reasons.

Foreword

My response to Jack Waugh's *20 Good Reasons to Study the Civil War* is Amen!

I believe, as does he, that every American should take the time to understand what happened among us those few years ago. It was the only time in our history that we took aim at each other and butchered each other in an organized way. One group of us put on dark blue uniforms, took up arms and fired at eyeball level at another group of us dressed in gray. And vice versa.

The brutality of our conflict was on par with that of most other wars of history. It turns out that we are not that different after all. Properly motivated, each of us Americans is also capable of committing barbaric acts, not only against a foreign enemy but against each other.

That, to me, is the major lesson of the Civil War. It is a lesson each of us, as we mount our occasional high-ground horses to preach morality and civility to others in the world, must know—and remember. It does not diminish the goodness and honor of us as a people and a nation, but it does offer perspective and, possibly, some humility.

In short, none of us Americans can really know ourselves completely unless we know the Civil War.

You don't have to take my words for it. Take Jack Waugh's. His ring with urgency and eloquence.

Jim Lehrer
Anchor, *PBS NewsHour*
Author, *No Certain Rest,* a novel of Antietam

Introduction

I discovered early in life that my reason for studying the American past and loving it so was the same reason a mountaineer climbs a mountain: Because it is there. That fantastic past has always been there for me, looming mountain-like and mesmeric, calling me to climb. It has been a call I have never resisted and never regretted. The climb has always been exhilarating.

Also early on, I found that of all the peaks in that mountainous past the one that called me most strongly was the Civil War era. Its drama, its pathos, its ironies, its people have made tremendous statements to me. For most of my career I was a newspaper journalist. But in that long career I was also a closet historian. Fifteen years ago I decided that I would come out of the closet, so to speak, and stop reporting the twentieth century and start reporting the nineteenth. This is the eighth book of my nineteenth-century career.

It seems appropriate, therefore, to write this slim volume of twenty reasons to study that war. They are by no means the only reasons. They are only twenty reasons that resonate with me. But they are good reasons that I hope will resonate with you and that, like me, you will find the mountain mesmeric and the climb exhilarating.

John C. Waugh
Arlington, Texas

REASON ONE
Because It Was Unique

If events in history could be called Wonders of the Past—as seven magnificent man-made spectaculars of antiquity were called Wonders of the World—the American Civil War would doubtless be one of them.

The Civil War was to history the equivalent of a wonder of the world, a towering passage in the human experience that would rival such man-made wonders as the Great Pyramid, the Sphinx, the Colossus of Rhodes, or the Hanging Gardens of Babylon. Like them, the Civil War excites awe. It was not beautiful, as those great wonders were. It was bloody, violent, and heartbreaking, a disaster in its toll of human lives, in the anguish and sorrow it left in its track, in its political, social, and emotional upheaval.

But it also ultimately brought "a new birth of freedom"—and over time national healing and better lives for succeeding generations of Americans, black and white. We became, because of the Civil War, a new nation, "a more perfect Union," closer-knit and more united than we had been before.

It has no parallel in the past. As Robert Penn Warren has written, the Civil War is, "for the American imagination, the great single event of our history." For four long bloody years—from April 1861 to June 1865—Americans fought Americans. Every Minié ball, every shot, every shell, every blast of canister, every war-linked disease that killed a man killed an American. That great war took 620,000 American lives—more than all other wars in our history combined. It savaged a generation of our young and brightest men. Every day on average more than 400 Americans died in the Civil War, seventeen an hour every day for four years. Such a loss of Americans in one day in any modern war would set off an outcry of anguish, protest, and sorrow that would destroy an administration. In the war in Iraq in 2003, a handful of American lives lost in a day, or a single life saved— the dramatic raid that rescued twenty-year-old Private Jessica Lynch comes to mind—riveted media-wide attention. But on the banks of the Antietam in September 1862, the single bloodiest day of the Civil War, 23,000 Americans were killed, wounded, or missing (whatever rescues there were went generally unreported). Daily death numbers such as those would paralyze government and media alike today.

That Americans were fighting and killing other Americans on such a devastating scale is unique in our history.

Yet just as unique were why the war was being fought and what was at stake. For five decades before the outbreak of the war at Fort Sumter in mid-April 1861, the nation had been dividing over the issue of slavery. When President Thomas Jefferson bought the Louisiana Purchase from Napoleon in 1803 he acquired a vast new territory out of which new states would one day be carved. Jefferson paid $15 million dollars for it and it doubled the size of the country overnight. But it was not an unalloyed bargain. It also created a crisis—an open wound that would fester for the next half century and finally bring civil war. At issue was whether slavery would be permitted to spread into new territory acquired by the government, a right demanded by the slaveholding South, or whether it must be kept slave-free, as demanded by the increasingly strident abolitionist North. Southerners heatedly threatened secession if they were not granted what they saw as their natural and constitutional right. They feared that if most of that territory eventually came into the Union as a phalanx of free states, a likely outcome, then the delicate balance of political power in the national government, their only bulwark against a rising abolitionist tide in the North, would be destroyed—and with it the Southern way of life. The fires of that initial crisis over the Louisiana Purchase territory were finally banked in 1820 in a famous compromise when Missouri—part of the Louisiana acquisition—was admitted to the Union as a slave state, balanced by the admission of Maine as a free state.

But tempers continued to fray. And thirty years later, in 1850, the issue over slavery in the territories and its attendant issue of the fast-eroding political balance of power broke out into an open crisis once again. Again it was triggered by another acquisition of a vast tract of land—the territories of California, New Mexico, and Utah—won in the war with Mexico in 1846-1848. A rerun of the Missouri crisis of 1820 resurfaced, ratcheted to a yet more intense pitch by ever more bitter Southern threats of secession and disunion if Southern rights were not protected. Only after nine months of explosive debate in the national Congress finally brought another famous compromise, were the fires of disunion again quenched.

But again, as it turned out, the compromise was but an armistice. Finally, by 1861, after another decade of rising tension over slavery, yet another compromise to still the tempest became impossible. Eleven Southern states seceded, the die was finally cast, and civil war came. In the Southern mind secession had become the only way to protect slavery and the Southern way of life against Northern abolitionist aggression and a Northern-dominated government in which they no longer had an equal voice.

There is yet another very important and unique thing—among many unique things—about our Civil War, and that was its incredible ironies. On the battlefields of the war it was possible that a Union soldier might turn over the body of a dead Confederate and see there the face of a brother or a son; or a Confederate soldier might find a mortally wounded Federal soldier dying on the battlefield and recognize in him a neighbor from home. After the battle of Bull Run, or First Manassas, two wounded brothers, one in blue, one in gray, who had not seen one another for years found themselves lying side-by-side in a stable-turned-hospital. In March 1862 Franklin Buchanan, flag officer of the Confederate ironclad *CSS Virginia*, rammed and captured the *USS Congress* on which his brother was the paymaster. Such ironies abound in the war.

Thousands of hearthsides, particularly in the border states—Virginia, Tennessee, Kentucky, Maryland, and Missouri—were shattered by domestic disunion. Families and neighbors were divided in sentiment and went to war against one another for their disparate beliefs. Three brothers of John Gibbon, a Union general, fought for the Confederacy. When George Thomas, another Union general, went with the Union against his native Virginia, his sisters turned his picture to the wall and never turned it back.

It was a war that divided not only minds, but hearts. And some men followed their hearts. Samuel Cooper was a New Yorker, the adjutant general of the Old Army. But his wife was a Virginian, the sister of James Mason, a United States senator before the war and then a noted Confederate diplomat. And one of Cooper's best friends was Jefferson Davis. Cooper went with the Confederacy as its adjutant general, its senior officer, outranking even Robert E. Lee until the war's closing weeks. John Pemberton, a Pennsylvanian who also married a Virginian, went, like Cooper, with the Confederacy and became one of its highest ranked officers, commanding, and finally surrendering the Confederate army defending Vicksburg in July 1863.

These heart-followings were a two-way street. Robert Anderson, the famed officer who commanded the Union garrison at Fort Sumter at the outbreak of the war, was a Kentuckian, a slave holder with Southern sentiments, married to a Georgian. Nonetheless, he held the Union dearer in his heart than all of this and remained faithful to it at Fort Sumter and then as a Union brigadier in the war that followed.

Poignant, gut wrenching irony was everywhere in the Civil War and it made for a passage of history that can only be called unique, one of the wonders of the past.

REASON TWO
Because It Was a Watershed in American History

By the outbreak of the Civil War, seven decades had passed since the young republic had became a nation of united yet separate states and elected its first president. But the mold still hadn't hardened, the cement hadn't set.

The United States was very much still a work in progress in 1861, its success and permanence by no means assured or guaranteed. George Washington, the first president to take the helm in 1789, steered the new ship with a cautious compass in his two terms in the highest office of the new nation. Being the first he was setting precedents that would need to stand the test of time if his young country were to survive. For much of those first seventy years, as fifteen other presidents succeeded him in turn, the Union stood on shaky ground. A renewed war with Great Britain in 1812-1815 saw the nation's existence again threatened from without. The capital at Washington, D.C., was seized, burned, and briefly occupied. One growing pain after another—economic, social, and political—succeeded. Problems inherent in creating a new nation rose to challenge its leaders. And always underneath, coiling and uncoiling like a serpent, as the great Civil War historian Bruce Catton has eloquently described it, was the slavery issue.

By the eve of the Civil War the national mixture, mainly because of that issue writhing under all, simply hadn't jelled. And until it did the Union would continue walking a tightrope between success and failure, between union and disunion.

The great men who founded this unique experiment in self government understood the problem. Many of them were not only great of mind, but great of body. George Washington stood six-feet two-inches tall, a giant in his time. Standing shoulder to shoulder and head to head with him, just as giant-sized, was that red headed thinker and polymath, Thomas Jefferson, who articulated for us the idea of independence. A much later president, John F. Kennedy, was to tell a meeting of Nobel Laureates at a White House dinner nearly two centuries after independence that such a show of brain power had not gathered there since Jefferson had dined alone. And Abraham Lincoln, a man of equal brilliance with Jefferson, who would be at the helm when the acid test of Civil War came, was six feet four. It seemed that in times of greatest need the people sent literal giants to lead us.

It has become apparent with the benefit of hindsight that until the issue of slavery and threatened disunion that hovered about it was settled one way or the other, the mix would never harden. The political union would never become a union of heart and mind, hence a true, permanent, and successful republic. Some men of vision saw it clearly even then. Lincoln, saw it. He said, in an immortal speech at Springfield, Illinois in June 1858 that in his opinion the nation would not become that union of heart and mind, hence permanent, until the agitation over slavery had ceased. And he believed it would not cease "until a crisis shall have been reached, and passed." A house divided against itself, he said, cannot stand. Lincoln said he believed "this government cannot endure, permanently half slave and half free." He said he did "not expect the Union to be dissolved—I do not expect the house to fall—but I do expect it will cease to be divided. It will become all one thing, or all the other." Lincoln well knew that until the republic became all one thing or all the other, its permanence was not assured. And on that belief he would be willing to lead the nation through a terrible fratricidal civil war to make it permanent.

Now, nearly a century and a half later, we understand—and historians often say—that what we were going through in the Civil War was nothing short of the event in our history that truly defined the United States as a nation. It changed the course of our history. There were great events in our past before the Civil War—the Revolution itself, bringing independence, and the War of 1812 when independence was again threatened. And there have been great events since that have challenged and tempered and matured us—the Industrial Revolution, the Great Depression, two world wars, the Cold War, a series of military police actions, and finally the technological revolution of today that is not only redefining us, but redefining the planet. But without that critical mid-course adjustment that was the Civil War, we would not have become what we have since become.

The Civil War is the dividing line in the timeline of U.S. history. When I was in college, some decades ago, the history textbooks naturally divided our past into two parts—the first part covering our history up through the Civil War, the second part beginning with Reconstruction and all of our history since. That dividing line is still there, and still there because it is such an obvious watershed—such a logical Rubicon in our history. It will always be seen as such. There may be other critical breaking points, but that one will always stand as the first great and critical one, surely the most critical. On its outcome everything since has rested.

It has not been easy becoming what we have become. We have struggled with the ramifications and fallout of that war ever since, wrestling relentlessly with a bitter aftertaste. In some minds the war is still being fought, its outcome bitterly resented. Many Southerners still find it hard reconciling to the truth that Lincoln won the war. We have since struggled over and over—indeed are still struggling—with race problems that snake back to slavery. We have labored ever since to replace slavery with racial equality. We have made strides. But it has taken another century and a half and it is still an unfinished work. Prejudice and inequality still exist in our Union.

But understanding the Civil War and what it meant, what it did to define us as a nation, is at the center of understanding who we are. That is not an original thought with me. Many historians have said it. Zachary Taylor, one of our presidents not as successful as some of the others, and dying in office in the middle of the crisis of 1850, said, "In my judgment, dissolution [of the Union] would be the greatest of calamities, and to avert that should be the study of every American. Upon its preservation must depend our own happiness and that of countless generations to come."

How it was to be preserved was indeed the study of every great American of Taylor's time. How it was finally preserved—though only by bloody and tragic civil war—is still the proper study of every American and will be so for generations to come.

REASON THREE
Because It Was a War of Firsts

War, like life, is a mixed pot of good and evil. The evil is what Lincoln might have described as "the better angels of our nature" gone bad. Men die in war. Youth is lost. Hearthsides are darkened. Lives are saddened and disrupted and economies are shattered. What generations have spent decades building are destroyed. And things afterward are never as they were before.

But war also has a perverse way of propelling us toward progress that might never have come without it—or would have come much more slowly. War is generally accompanied by an upwelling of inventiveness. Some of the most astonishing and positive new advances arise out of war. Many of these firsts are not pretty. Many of them are designed to maim and kill. But many of them have lasting impacts—and often more constructive uses—that far outlive the war itself.

The Civil War, perhaps more than most, was a war of firsts. And to see these firsts emerging—many of them leading to things we can't now envision living without—we must return to that war.

For the first time in any war there was conscription—on both sides—a Secret Service, an income tax, a withholding tax, and a tobacco and cigarette tax, wigwag signal codes, photography on a battlefield, an African-American army officer, the Medal of Honor, and a trumpet call called "Taps." The first flares were sent aloft to light a battlefield at night. And for the first time in our history a president was assassinated.

The railroad, riding the tide of the industrial revolution, was new-born in the nineteenth century. By the eve of the war more than 30,000 miles of rails had been stitched down across the country, most of them east of the Mississippi, and two thirds of them in the North. An intercontinental railroad from coast to coast was the dream of ambitious industrialists and politicians before the war. And after it the same engineers who had laid the rails for the armies in the war, would make that dream a reality, linking the country forever and irrevocably from sea to shining sea.

The telegraph was another exciting new fact of life by the mid-nineteenth century. It was already linking major cities in the country before the war. But it hadn't yet become omnipresent or mobile. Not until Union General George B. McClellan dragged a telegraph line behind him on the battle-fields in western Virginia early in the war, was its potential for instantaneous communication between people wherever they were and whatever they were doing realized. A Confederate soldier, taken prisoner in McClellan's victorious western Virginia campaign in the early summer of 1861, saw the telegraph line snaking out of McClellan's headquarters and exclaimed to a fellow prisoner, "My God, Jim, no wonder they whipped us; they have the telegraph with them."

It was an important first, the forerunner of other ever more startling means of permitting people to communicate instantly with one another, though miles, even continents apart. Not many steps or much time separated this advance from the telephone, the radio, television, and in our time the world wide Internet with its web sites and chat rooms and instantaneous e-mail that are truly making one world of our planet.

For the first time in the midst of any civil war anytime anywhere, a presidential election was conducted. It was democracy at work, proving itself despite the gunfire, a triumph of the ballot over the bullet, a fantastic first in world history. It had never happened before and wasn't likely to happen often again. And for the first time in any war, soldiers voted in the field in an election campaign. Not until the Civil War did a soldier go off to war and not lose his franchise. Always before the only place a soldier could legally vote in any state was at his home polling place. When the war came no legislation existed in any state that permitted voting anywhere but there. Wisconsin and Minnesota were the first states to break from this rule and permit their citizen-soldiers to vote in the field. By 1864, in the presidential election, thirteen states allowed voting in the field. Four other states had laws permitting soldiers to vote from the seat of war by proxy. Only five Northern states by then required soldiers to come home if they wished to vote. This simple adjustment in the franchise was a giant step forward in the evolution of democratic government. It was a notable first.

For the first time in any war, gas-filled balloons were lofted into the sky to spy on an enemy. Reconnaissance from on high by aeronauts was not the safest venue for a human being, for it gave birth to the first ever antiaircraft fire. It gave birth as well to the first blackouts and camouflage on the ground below. And there was the problem of getting what those first aeronauts' eyes saw of value from the air back to earth with or without themselves. Taking a page from McClellan in the field, air-to-land telegraph wires were tried, but often failed to survive liftoff. These aeronauts of the Civil War in their observation balloons roughly and tentatively pointed the way to manned flight and to the technically sophisticated unmanned observation and communication from the stratosphere and from the universe beyond that we know today.

Medicine in the Civil War was rudimentary, undeveloped, and often deadly in itself. The number one antidote for a ghastly wound was a ghastly amputation under ghastly unsanitary conditions. But in many ways the sheer coping with the wounds and with man-maiming disease—which killed more men in the war than shot and shell—forced the medical arts out of the medieval ages and set them on a course to what we now know as modern medicine. For the first time in any war there were hospital ships, an organized medical and nursing corps—and an ambulance corps to carry the wounded and dying to them. The war gave birth as well, out of the desperate need to lessen pain, to the first widespread use of anesthetics and to the pharmaceutical industry that would revolutionize medicine in the twentieth and twenty-first centuries.

From such Civil War firsts—and so many others, whether designed for killing or for healing—we have harvested many of the things which, sublimated to a higher use, now ease our labors, lessen our pain, and save our lives.

REASON FOUR
Because it Saved Republican Government

At stake in our Civil War was not only the life of our Union, but perhaps even more critical, the life of a form of government unique in the world. At stake was the question of whether republican government, such a new idea in world history, could survive a life-threatening political and military crisis from within.

Could such a form of government—a nation "of the people, by the people, and for the people"—surmount this deadly threat and not perish from the earth? The very life of this different form of government, as Abraham Lincoln knew and so eloquently stated, was at stake in the war. If this unique experiment in self-government could not survive such a test here, where everything was new, where tyranny had not yet risen and the canvas was uncluttered, then representative government based on individual freedom and consent of the governed was not likely to be able to survive anywhere. The nations of the world in 1861, in general, were ruled by monarchs, dictators, overlords, and worse. The prevailing systems of government were not geared to, nor did they welcome, meaningful participation from the masses.

Whatever was driving others, survival of this central prize without price, representative government, was what the war was all about for Abraham Lincoln. He said it with an eloquence that still rings down the decades. In 272 of the most eloquent words ever uttered in the English language, on the casket-circled field at Gettysburg, Pennsylvania, in November 1863—three and a half months after the bloody battle on that field—Lincoln articulated this idea for the ages: "Four score and seven years ago our fathers brought forth on this continent a new nation, conceived in Liberty, and dedicated to the proposition that all men are created equal. Now we are engaged in a great civil war, testing whether that nation or any nation so conceived and so dedicated, can long endure."

That this government of the people, so dear to Lincoln, did not perish from the earth is the sublime fruit of that terrible war. It did endure. The Civil War settled the issue. But it was a close call. That it survived is alone reason enough to make the Civil War one of the great critical passages in world history, and worthy of everlasting study.

If the South had successfully sheared from the Union and set up business on its own, the split might have permanently balkanized the North American continent. The possible train of events that would follow such an outcome are well known and unthinkable—internecine wars, raids across borders, weakness in the face of foreign aggressors, a tangle of tariffs, crippled economies that fail to mesh, the politics of upheaval, lower standards of living. We would never have become a world leader and the beacon of hope and the haven of charity and democracy that we have become on this planet.

Lincoln well knew that the price to prevent that misery and save republican government came high. But that he considered it worth the cost is clearly evident in the fact that he sent men to war knowing that thousands of them would never return. For him it was worth dying for, indeed he himself would die for it with a bullet in his brain fired by an assassin in a theater in Washington in the spring of 1865. On the field at Gettysburg in a brief, immortal two-minute speech Lincoln in 1863 spoke of those brave men "who here gave their lives that that nation might live." He clearly understood how high the stakes were and how high the price. And, although grieved that it must be so, he knew it must be paid. As he was to say in his equally eloquent second inaugural address in Washington a year and a half later, little more than a month before he died, one party in the conflict "would make war rather than let the nation survive; and the other would accept war rather than let it perish. And the war came." Lincoln understood that the cost of its coming in human lives would be appalling, but he believed that it nonetheless was a price worth the objective.

The idea that the Union was only meant to be a loose confederation of states, not an unbreakable union with a stronger, binding, higher national government, was an idea that lived on after the Revolutionary War and persisted still in the antebellum South in Civil War times. It was an idea the South had never given up. In Southern minds, state's rights were preeminent over national unity. Southerners cherished their states' autonomy. It was in character that the Confederacy named its armies in the war after states while the Union named its armies after rivers. Southerners were more comfortable with a state government that was only loosely joined under an umbrella government than they were with a strong Union that could force its will on the individual states. This idea of a loose confederacy had long been held and strongly persisted in the South up to and through the Civil War. For most Southerners their first allegiance was not to the United States but to their native states. Most of them were to act on that belief when Civil War came. Robert E. Lee and

Thomas J. "Stonewall" Jackson, those two preeminent Confederate generals, though they loved the Union and deplored slavery, could not bring themselves to raise their swords against their state of Virginia.

State's rights was the driving value that Southerners evoked to secede. The South always wanted that out, that looseness of confederation rather than the tightness of a binding nationhood under a higher central power. They saw that out as essential to preserving their way of life, to their right to own slaves, to their ability to run their individual states as they saw fit, without outside interference. They saw state's rights as their safe harbor from the mounting antislavery sentiment in the North, an aggressive sentiment that threatened everything that was important in the Southern mind. A stronger union meant a weaker state and a weaker state in the face of a huge population bulge in the North foretold doom for slavery and the Southern way of life and the economy based upon it. The only way out in many Southern minds was to secede and in effect kill the whole idea of union and republican government, just the opposite of what Lincoln held so dear and was sending Northern men into battle to die for.

It is perhaps the irony of ironies in the Civil War that the objective that the South sought with secession—preserving its way of life against a majority bent on destroying slavery—did just the opposite. The act of secession set the seal of death to the very system it was designed to save. The war that followed that rash act set the South back a generation or more across the board—in everything that sustains a region. The South reaped only disaster from the war and became for a time virtually an occupied territory. It was decades climbing out of that abyss.

Some far-sighted men saw this consequence at the time. James Louis Pettigru, a Southern lawyer, a member of the

Charleston elite and a South Carolina plantation owner and slave holder, saw it clearly, saw that secession from the Union would be tested in blood and the loser would be the South. He virtually stood alone among the men of his state, the first to secede, in seeing secession as a suicidal act and opposing it with heart, mind, and tongue. He is famous for throwing up his hands when his state seceded and exclaiming that South Carolina was too small to be a nation and too large for an insane asylum. Although he remained in South Carolina throughout the war, he was a pariah, never supporting the Confederacy. He had the vision to see beyond the war to what was really at stake—and indeed what was going to happen. He saw tragedy for the South where most Southerners saw salvation.

In the end, perhaps secession was necessary to the salvation of the successful experiment in representative government that Lincoln so treasured and would lay down lives to save. Seen in that light the test in blood of a civil war was something that had to come to shape a more permanent union.

REASON FIVE
Because It Killed Slavery

The Civil War in the beginning was not waged to destroy slavery, at least not in the mind of Lincoln and other moderate men of the time. Despite the rantings of the abolitionists, that goal was not the goal in the first years of the war. The central aim of the war in Lincoln's mind was to preserve the Union. It was, as he so clearly articulated it, to preserve this unique experiment in representative government.

Lincoln was prepared either to save or abolish slavery—whatever it took to save the Union. But never was the end of slavery seen by him as an end in itself. He believed when the war began that slavery, by constitutional requirement, was to be left alone in the states where it then existed. He was interested only in preventing it from expanding into the new territories. Personally Lincoln, thinking slavery wrong, deplored it. But whatever might ultimately happen to it, his higher priority was clearly saving the Union.

Lincoln wrote a letter in August 1862 to Horace Greeley, the contentious, eccentric, and abolitionist editor of the *New York Tribune*. Greeley had written Lincoln a public letter published in his paper under the title, "The Prayer of Twenty Millions" (the population of the North in the Civil War). In it, Greeley protested Lincoln's policies on slavery and demanded that he vigorously enforce the execution of the Confiscation Act freeing slaves.

In eloquent cadences that so marked his thinking and writing, Lincoln answered Greeley, in part: "I would save the Union. I would save it in the shortest way under the Constitution. The sooner the national authority can be restored; the nearer the Union will be 'the Union that it was.' If there be those who would not save the Union, unless they could at the same time *save* slavery, I do not agree with them. If there be those who would not save the Union, unless they could at the same time *destroy* slavery, I do not agree with them. My paramount object in this struggle is to save the Union, and is *not* either to save or to destroy slavery. If I could save the Union without freeing *any* slave I would do it, and if I could save it by freeing *all* the slaves I would do it; and if I could save it by freeing some and leaving others alone I would also do that. What I do about slavery, and the colored race, I do because I believe it helps to save the Union, and what I forbear, I forbear because I do *not* believe it would help to save the Union. I shall do *less* whenever I shall believe what I am doing hurts the cause, and I shall do *more* whenever I shall believe doing more will help the cause."

When he wrote this, Lincoln had already decided to draft and issue a proclamation of freedom for slaves when the time seemed appropriate. And he would do so, in a famed edict, the Emancipation Proclamation, issued after the battle of Antietam in September 1862, to take effect January 1, 1863. That document overnight turned the war into a war not just to save the Union but, indeed, to destroy slavery. Lincoln took this monumental step only after becoming convinced, with or without Greeley's letter, that an edict emancipating slaves in the South would indeed help the cause—more quickly end the rebellion and restore the Union.

For a long time many had believed that slavery in the long term was on the road to ultimate extinction, for it had died out virtually everywhere else in the world and was morally insupportable in any place. But before the Civil War it was believed the road to ultimate extinction would be longer rather than shorter, and by evolution rather than by revolution. The advent of the Civil War and Lincoln's proclamation changed all that. It put the extinction of slavery on a fast track, far faster than it would have been had the South not seceded. Again, what the South intended to accomplish with secession brought precisely the opposite outcome, and brought it in four years. The Emancipation Proclamation only freed slaves in those parts of Southern states still in Confederate hands. But it was a monumental act because it ended forever government support for slavery where it existed in the South and was to lead, by war's end, to the Thirteenth Amendment to the Constitution, which permanently outlawed slavery everywhere throughout the restored Union and its territories.

Slavery indeed died in the Civil War. Racism didn't and hasn't to this day. And there had to be two more amendments to the Constitution, numbers fourteen and fifteen, to begin to give the freed slave equal rights in his new-born freedom. But slavery, racism's most extreme manifestation, did die in the fire and fury of civil war. Its death, together with the saving of republican government, is clearly one of the two preeminent outcomes of the war of brothers.

REASON SIX
Because It Originated New Ways of Waging War

Warfare in many ways would never be the same after the American Civil War. The war became, for many reasons, a watershed in history and a watershed in the way war was to be waged then and in all future time.

New weaponry is always colliding with old ways of fighting, overnight rendering those old ways obsolete. War changed when clubs were replaced by spears and spears by arrows and arrows by crossbows and crossbows by bullets. Warfare made a radical jump when men substituted hurling boulders from awkward catapults to hurling shot and shell from the mouth of cannon. And to no less extent new weaponry appearing for the first time forced change, radical change, in strategy and tactics in the Civil War.

For the first time in warfare repeating rifles and carbines with grooved barrels were put into the hands of Civil War soldiers in lethal numbers. These newly developed and improved repeating weapons would change forever the way successful future wars would be fought on a battlefield. Repeating rifles and carbines, capable of firing one shot after another without reloading and with greater accuracy at longer distances, made the single shot smooth-bore muzzle-loading muskets that dominated at the war's beginning obsolete by the war's end. They also made traditional tactics of massed frontal charges against

well-defended ramparts obsolete. Rarely after the Civil War—
after massed charges at Gettysburg mauled the Confederate
divisions of George Pickett, James Pettigrew, and Isaac R.
Trimble, and at Cold Harbor where more than 5000 Union soldiers were gunned down or lost in half a day—would "attack and
die" tactics be a viable way to wage war. Yet that was how war
had been waged for centuries.

No less striking than the repeating rifle and carbine was the
evolution of artillery. Just as the rifled musket barrel made soldier-
to-soldier fighting on a battlefield more deadly than ever before,
rifled artillery, newly emerging and complementing the more
common smooth-bore cannon, made killing en mass at longer
ranges with greater accuracy more telling than ever before and
foreshadowed the massive firepower of the artillery of the future.

As the means of killing became more deadly they also
became more versatile and innovative. The Civil War saw
artillery fired for the first time from flatbed railroad cars. The
first land-mine fields, the first wire entanglements, the first
rudimentary flame throwers, the first telescopic sight, the first
revolving gun turret, the first fundamental but workable
machine gun, which Lincoln called the "coffee-mill gun"—all
date from the Civil War.

But it was not just the revolution in the tools of killing that
changed the face of war. Just as important was the concept of
what the overall strategy of the war ought to be—and the phi-
losophy by which it should be waged. For that we have to revisit the modus operandi of that eccentric flame-haired Union
general, William Tecumseh Sherman. For the concept of "total
war" that he embraced—and practiced—in the hell and fury of
the Civil War was to become the Open Sesame that would finally seal the fate of the South and hasten the end of the war to an
ultimate Northern victory.

As new weaponry wrenched war away from old ways of fighting, Sherman sharply sheared away from the way war had been seen and fought for centuries, a static affair with one side lining up in packed rank and charging a packed rank of the enemy. Sherman cut loose from his base of supplies and resources in 1864 after the fall of Atlanta, and put his great army in motion. As it marched it lived off the enemy's land—itself an innovation for the times, since armies were traditionally followed by long wagon trains of equipment and supplies. Sherman's idea in casting off and marching across Georgia after the fall of Atlanta was to "make Georgia howl!" In his famous—or notorious—march from Atlanta to Savannah and the sea, he cut a sixty-mile wide swath of destruction across the state and indeed made it howl. Sherman said, "war is war and not popularity-seeking." Nor did he win popularity in his march to the sea—not in the South at any rate. Many Southerners have not to this day forgotten nor have they forgiven.

It was not the first time this kind of unforgiving warfare had been practiced. Armies ancient and not so ancient had used it or attempted to use it before. Nor would it be the last. In World War II the Germans adopted it and called it *blitzkrieg.*

But it was a kind of warfare that went wildly against everything about war that Southerners considered civilized. Southerners valued chivalry in battle. But there was little chivalry in Sherman's way of waging war. No longer was the Union army treating the enemy's country and civilian population with restraint. Sherman had decided if the South was to be beaten and the rebellion put down, then its people and its land, not just its soldiers, must suffer. He believed the Southern will to continue in rebellion must be broken. And he was to break it by wielding terror against Southern civilians—not killing, but the destruction of property—as a weapon. "My aim," he said, "was to whip the rebels, to humble their pride, to follow them in their inmost recesses, and make them fear and dread us."

It was not, ironically, that Sherman hated the South or Southerners. Quite the opposite. He brought total war to the South as a tool to end the rebellion. But it was not personal with Sherman, who before the war had lived in the South—in Louisiana—and liked and admired Southerners, and harbored pro-slavery sentiments. After waging uncompromising total war against the South, Sherman at war's end took the surrender of the Confederate army under his friend Joseph E. Johnston in North Carolina. Believing it was what Lincoln, now assassinated, would have wished, Sherman offered peace terms striking for their forgiving leniency. They were far too lenient for the far more hard-hearted Secretary of War Edwin Stanton—and even U.S. Grant. Stanton saw them as entirely too soft on the rebels and, with Lincoln gone, took the lead in seeing them retracted.

The war threw up strange paradoxes. And It also brought strategic and tactical revolution with the rebellion. And no revolution was more telling than the evolution it brought to the ways of waging war.

REASON SEVEN
Because It Revolutionized War on the Water

Often in the war, before Northern fortunes finally turned, Abraham Lincoln had cause to despair of the progress of Union arms on land. His army in the East in the first two years suffered hard setbacks—at First and Second Manassas, on the Peninsula, at Fredericksburg and Chancellorsville.

By contrast, Lincoln often had cause in the war to rejoice to news from his ships at sea and his gunboats on the rivers. In late August 1863, when fortune was finally turning for the North after Gettysburg and Vicksburg, he wrote fondly of "Uncle Sam's Web-feet." They must not be forgotten, he said. "At all the watery margins they have been present. Not only on the deep sea, the broad bay, and the rapid river, but also up the narrow muddy bayou, and wherever the ground was a little damp, they have been, and made their tracks."

Lincoln's Secretary of the Navy, Gideon Welles, was old-foggyish, with a flowing white beard that caused Lincoln to call him "Father Neptune." But more often than not in the war Father Neptune brought Lincoln good tidings—of Admiral David Farragut's spectacular running of the forts at New Orleans in 1862 and Mobile Bay in 1864, and other news of good fortune on the bays and seas edging the continent and on the broad rivers that cut the continent and divided the armies. When the exultant Welles hurried to the White House in July 1863, and uncharacteristically did a double-shuffle and threw his hat before telling Lincoln that he had a message from Admiral David Porter on the scene that Vicksburg had surrendered to Grant, Lincoln, nearly hugged him. "What can we do for the Secretary of the Navy for this glorious intelligence?" Lincoln exclaimed. "He is always giving us good news."

More than good news was coming from the water. A sea-change in naval warfare was transpiring on the oceans and the rivers of the war—as dramatic in its way as the changing face of war on land. New technology was already transforming war on the water even before the rebellion. The steam engine, the screw propeller, more powerful ordnance were already signaling the birth of a new era in naval warfare. The Civil War would bring these and other innovations to the front in a mighty rush.

From the beginning when Lincoln ordered a naval blockade of the more than 3,500-mile Southern coastline, there developed a running need to change and adapt on both sides. New ways of hunting and chasing down blockade-running boats, and new ways for those hunted boats to camouflage themselves in ocean-blending gray, sleek down, and slip silently past and outrun the hunters became necessary. On the high seas commerce raiding was raised to a fine art by such bold Confederate cruisers as *CSS Alabama* and *CSS Florida*..

Innovation was evident everywhere on the water. On March 9, 1862 there was an epic battle at Hampton Roads in Virginia—between two ships with iron sides. One was a Federal frigate called *Merrimac* that had been burned to the gunwales, and seized and refitted by Confederates with iron plates and a ramming horn and renamed *Virginia*. The other was a newly designed low-lying Union vessel named *Monitor* that looked like a raft, with a revolving gun turret on her flat deck that

resembled a hat box. These two unique iron-bound boats—
Monitor and *Merrimac*—fought to an epic four-hour standoff at
Hampton Roads in that battle in 1862. It was no ordinary bench-
mark in naval history. It was a revolution. In that four hours the
two ironclads had made obsolete every wooden-hulled ship-of-
war in the water everywhere and changed naval warfare forever.

Innovation was also bringing change under the water.
Rudimentary submarines were developed and floated for the
first time in the Civil War. Only one, *CSS Hunley*, converted from
a 25-foot-long boiler tank, devised by the Confederacy and
called the "Fish Boat," succeeded in sinking an enemy vessel in
combat. And *Hunley* with her crew of eight was, as all such
crude experiments in submersible vessels then were, the devil
to maneuver and suicidal to man. When *Hunley* sank the Union
sloop-of-war, USS *Housatonic*, in February 1864, she also sank,
taking her crew to the bottom several miles from her victim. But
from this fundamental and lethal beginning we got the far more
deadly convoy-stalking, ship-sinking U-boats and submarines
in the two world wars and the sophisticated nuclear subs of
today capable of laying waste to continents.

There was yet another species of underwater demon born of
the war, called torpedoes. They were rudimentary floating
mines suspended from lines anchored to the muddy bottoms of
waters threatened by invading fleets. The torpedoes were
exploded either electronically or by percussion, and they didn't
always detonate when brushed by the hulls of the passing vessels they were designed to sink. But they succeeded often
enough to rip gaping holes in unsuspecting keels and send
more than one gunboat or monitor or warship to the bottom.
They in no way resembled the deadly swift-running torpedoes
of later naval wars, cutting through the water on unerring paths
toward the keels of unsuspecting victims. But they pointed the

way to the havoc their more sophisticated and powerful underwater descendents would one day bring.

The nation's rivers, in particular the Mississippi, as mighty in its own way as the open sea, also hosted innovation. Hulking river boats, as long as half a football field, clad in iron, and moving like giant turtles on the water, were sent with great effect up and down the navigable rivers to augment and support the armies that were fighting along their banks. Union generals in particular frequently had occasion to be grateful for these ironclad river boats commanded by their naval counterparts. The boats were major players in the war career of U.S. Grant, who saw them make a huge difference on the Tennessee and Cumberland Rivers at Forts Henry and Donelson, and on the Mississippi in his long hard conquest of Vicksburg. *CSS Tennessee*, a Confederate ironclad ram designed to go to sea, was a protagonist in one of the epic naval battles of the war in Mobile Bay in August 1864.

The pioneering advances that the war produced on the water would be long felt. As the weapons that transformed fighting on land were the forerunners of a new kind of terrestrial warfare, these changes on the rivers and the seas were harbingers of the naval might of World Wars I and ll.

REASON EIGHT
Because It Teaches Us Brotherhood

In the summer of 1864 George McClellan, who had commanded the Union armies early in the war, returned to West Point, his alma mater, to deliver the speech at the dedication of the ground set aside for a monument to the regular Union officers and men who had died in the war.

There McClellan spoke of the "sacred brotherhood of arms" that bound West Pointers. It was a powerful concept, that brotherhood of arms, and it held tenaciously throughout the war, binding the hearts of enemies who were fighting one another. We have never seen brotherhood stretched so far, absorb such blows, pass through such fire, and survive so intact as in the Civil War. It was love so strong, so heart-embedded, that it could transcend even a vicious fratricidal war.

Many of these men who wound up fighting one another in the war were dearest of friends. Many, like McClellan, had been West Pointers and had been classmates and roommates at the Academy. They had served side-by-side in the Mexican War and in the antebellum Indian wars in Florida and on the plains of the American West. They been groomsmen at one another's weddings. They had loved one another. And when Civil War came and they had to chose higher allegiances and fight one another, they parted, grasping hands one more time, speaking farewells that they feared would be forever, many with tears in their eyes.

But in their hearts through all the killing of the Civil War the love lived on and it made for the most ironic of wars. The outpourings of brotherly affection between enemies that the war produced are legion.

When George Pickett, a Confederate general, heard that George McClellan, commanding Union armies, was ill in the Peninsula, he grieved, hoping that it was not life-threatening, for though McClellan was the enemy, he loved him. When it was reported to Union generals who had been his friends in the Old Army that Pickett and his new bride, LaSalle, had had a baby boy, they sent a birthday gift to him across the lines. When Confederate General Richard S. Ewell, then a prisoner in a Union prison, heard of the death of Abraham Lincoln whose armies had put him there, he wept.

When George McClellan died and was laid to rest in New Jersey in 1885, former Confederate generals came to mourn his passing. When U.S. Grant died that same year, Confederate generals wearing their gray sashes, enemies in the war, sadly followed his casket. Among them was Joseph E. Johnston, who by then had already performed pall-bearing services for many of his former Union enemies and fellow generals. When William Sherman, the man who had defeated him and taken his surrender at the end of the war, died in 1891, Johnston, who would himself be dead little more than a month later, was at his graveside, chief among the mourners.

Often in the evenings in the war as the armies lay across a river or across a battlefield from one another, regimental bands of both armies would strike up and the soldiers in blue and gray would sit and listen together to tunes they all knew and shared in common. Such concerts often ended in a mournful rendering of that good-night song of the soul, "Home Sweet Home." And all the soldiers on both sides would sing it together and often weep to it together. It was "the better angels of our nature" raised in a common song and speaking enemy to enemy and heart to heart. There was indeed a brotherhood of arms and it was, as McClellan said, sacred.

REASON NINE
Because It Showcases Undaunted Courage

Few of us know beforehand how we might act when we first "see the elephant." Comparing battle to seeing the elephant was an apt analogy. For few living animals come bigger on earth or more hugely and uniquely different than an elephant. And few things are more fierce and terrifying than battle. Do we show bravery, or cowardice in the face of it? Do we advance, even in a blizzard of bullets, or do we turn and run?

Soldiers in the Civil War did both. It seemed, as Horace Porter, one of Grant's staff officers, wrote some years after the war, that "courage, like most other qualities, is never assured until it has been tested. No man knows precisely how he will behave in battle until he has been under fire." There were many cowards who, tested, could not endure the sight of the elephant. But there were many more who, seeing it, drew on something within that was greater than the fear of death and showed incredible courage. We study the Civil War to learn about both, but we study it mostly to learn of the greatness of the human spirit. There is no more telling teaching ground for that than the Civil War.

Lincoln himself, thinking of battle but not ever having been in one, speculated that he might turn and run. But when Lincoln did come under fire in war time, the first sitting president ever to do so, he showed unflinching courage. He stood on a parapet at Fort

Stevens in the Washington suburbs in the summer of 1864 and watched with seeming unconcern as Confederate sniper bullets whizzed about him, felling an officer standing by his side. When Captain Oliver Wendell Holmes, the future great Supreme Court justice, saw him looming there against the sky, a rich target for a bullet, he shouted "Get down you fool!" It was no way to talk to the commander-in-chief—and it may have really happened, or been but a figment of Holmes's aging memory. But with it and the urgings of the Union general commanding on the scene Lincoln did get down, but only reluctantly.

Lincoln that day proved himself not a coward. He also showed day to day courage throughout the war, being wholly unafraid to venture out alone, an open unguarded target for an assassin. Again only reluctantly did he submit to a cavalry escort to and from his summer retreat outside of Washington. On one occasion when a shot went through his stove pipe hat he made light of it. He understood and was resigned to the fact that anybody wanting to take his life could do it whether he went guarded or unguarded.

Yet not being a coward, Lincoln nonetheless had a liberal heart where cowardice had been shown in others. He did not necessarily blame a young man for caving in to his natural instinct for self-preservation in the face of the elephant. Lincoln was noted—notorious in the view of some of his generals—for reversing their orders to execute men who had done the cowardly thing in battle. Loving a good joke, he told the one about the Irish soldier who, when asked why he had deserted, replied, "Well, Captain, it was not me fault. I've a heart in me breast as brave as Julius Caesar; but when the battle begins, somehow or other these cowardly legs of mine will run away wid me!"

Whether a man is courageous or whether he is a coward, whether he stands or his cowardly legs take him away, there is an instinct that causes most men, even the most courageous, to dodge and feint involuntarily under a heavy hail of infantry fire. Porter believed that only the bravest of the brave do not flinch. He could recall, in all his years at the seat of war, seeing only two men who throughout a rattling musketry fire sat in their saddles without moving a muscle or blinking an eye. One was a bugler in the regular cavalry and the other was U.S. Grant. Grant's soldiers often saw this and marveled. One of his soldiers said of him, "Ulysses don't scare worth a damn."

Confederate General "Stonewall" Jackson was cut from the same cloth. William B. Taliaferro, one of Jackson's brigadiers for a time, tells the story of Jackson in the Shenandoah Valley superintending his artillery fire amid a rain of bullets. Oblivious to the iron storm raging about him, Jackson was busily assessing the effect his guns were having on the enemy. In the midst of all this lethal chaos, Jackson turned to a very nervous Taliaferro and asked, offhandedly, as if passing the time of day in a rocker on the front porch, "Are you a family man, General?" Taliaferro answered: "I have a wife and five children at home, and my impression is that in less than five minutes there will be a widow and five orphans there."

The courage of a Grant or a Jackson was a courage they shared with virtually all West Pointers. General George Patton, the hero-general of World War II and a West Pointer, once said that you could not find a coward among them. The reason: they would rather die than appear cowards before their peers.

Even if a soldier did cut and run, where was he to go on a bullet-raked battlefield that was any safer than where he was? Horace Porter told the story of the soldier who was hunkered down with the rest of his regiment under heavy fire and under cover of rolling ground. After so much of this the soldier snapped under the strain and, no longer able to endure it, sprang to his feet and started for the rear. He soon found himself in a level field being plowed by shot and shell and far less safe than the ground he had just left. "What are you doing there?" demanded an officer. "Well, said the man, "I'm looking for the rear of this army, but it don't seem to have any."

For courage unmatched, in which the Civil War abounds, we must look to the common soldier of both sides. We must look at the Confederate soldiers, who without question and without hesitating, made the suicidal charge across two-thirds of a mile of open ground for Robert E. Lee on the third day at Gettysburg through a blizzard of shot and shell and musket fire. We must look to the federal soldiers before Cold Harbor, who saw what they must do the next morning, and pinned slips of paper with their names and home addresses in the seams of their coats so their friends in the battle and their families at home might know them dead. Such courage, Porter believed, "is more than heroic; it is sublime."

Sublime courage is there to see in that war at every turn. It is seen in the 1200 Medals of Honor awarded Union officers and men in the war and in the thousands of other acts of bravery that went unhonored by other non-cowards. And that mirrors only the courage on the Union side. Thousands of Rebels, upon seeing the elephant, rose to equal greatness.

After the war Oliver Wendell Holmes wrote: "Through our great good fortune in our youth our hearts were touched with fire. It was given us to learn at the outset that life is a profound and passionate thing. . . . But above all we have learned that whether a man accepts from Fortune her spade and will look downward and dig, or from Aspiration her axe and cord and will scale the ice, the one and only success which it is his to command is to bring to his work a mighty heart."

Many in the Civil War brought to it a mighty heart.

REASON TEN
Because It Made Heroes

Justice Holmes, a man of surpassing eloquence, said something else long after the war. He said, "Don't call me a hero. I trust I did my duty as a soldier respectably, but I was not born for it and did nothing remarkable in that way."

That is often the case with heroism. It is often at its most sublime when low key, without bravado, a matter-of-fact expression of human excellence. It was telling to me that movie makers who judge such things agreed not long ago that the greatest film hero in the history of motion pictures was not a Rambo or a Terminator or a gunslinger or a good cop or a superhero. The greatest hero of them all was a small-town Southern lawyer named Atticus Finch, the quiet unassuming father of two children, Scout (Jean Louise) and Jem, portrayed by Gregory Peck in "To Kill a Mockingbird." His courage was defending a black man wrongfully accused of raping a white woman in the racist South. When Atticus had done all he could to see justice done and failed and all the white folks in the courtroom had left, he slowly packed his papers in his brief case and started for the door.

In the gallery of the courtroom every black person who had been present at the trial was still there and all were standing, their hats in their hands. As Atticus walked by beneath, one of them said to Scout, who had been sitting with them and was still sitting, "Miss Jean Louse, Miss Jean Louise, stand up. Your father's passin'.'" It was a surpassing tribute to quiet, sublime heroism and one of the great moments in film history.

There were many moments such as this in the Civil War, when heroism spoke so quietly, often without notice, yet said great things.

Most of the heroes we associate with the Civil War bear the names of presidents and generals. They were the most visible of the heroes then and the most vivid in our memories now. They occupy a special pantheon in history. As a people we have an urgent need to know them and what they did. We are a person-ality-oriented society. And these star names from the Civil War—Abraham Lincoln, Jefferson Davis, Robert E. Lee, Stonewall Jackson, Nathan Bedford Forrest, U.S. Grant, William Tecumseh Sherman, Philip Sheridan, and many others North and South— were legend-makers and an inseparable part now of the American memory.

And all of them were not men. Thousands of women in the war rose to heights of heroism that only noble spirits can. Some became famous. Clara Barton, taking her love and compassion and healing skill to the battlefield, became a symbol in the war of caring and courageous womanhood. And she represented the hundreds like her of equal power and strength.

These heroes, men and women, are one of the main reasons we study the Civil War. They are the magnets, the magical names, that draw us to it.

Depending on which side your sentiments lie, some of these names may not be your heroes. But they were heroes nonethe-less—Jefferson Davis as much a hero in Southern memory as Lincoln is in Northern memory, Lee and Jackson and Forest as much heroes as Grant and Sherman and Sheridan. Time has blurred the distinctions. They were heroes because they were tested in the fire that touched them all and sublimated by what they did or tried to do. Not all of them were successful in the end, just as Atticus Finch was not successful. But they proved heroes by their mettle. Heroes more often than not are associated with success. But that is never the sole requirement. History is studded with heroes who did not succeed. Lincoln, Grant, Sherman, and Sheridan succeeded and won the war. Davis didn't succeed, didn't win the war, nor in the end did Lee nor Jackson nor Forrest. They are heroes nonetheless.

There were many of them, all tempered by the fire that touched them. Just as war throws up many new things out of necessity, these men became heroes out of necessity. Many Civil War heroes were, like Holmes, not born to war. Many were not natural soldiers. And part of their greatness is that they became heroes despite this. Many went to the war because it was the great event of their time. Not to be a part of it was unthinkable for many of them. It offered opportunity for distinction, which their ambitions eagerly sought. There was an absolute need to be there. The magnetism of the event was too powerful to resist. It drew them just as it draws us today. It was the defining event of their era. It is still the defining event of our past.

These heroes are role models for us even now, possessing character against which we can measure ourselves. They still show us, a century and a half later, the courage and nobility of which man is capable.

REASON ELEVEN
Because It Created a New Industrial America

When Abraham Lincoln spoke of the need for the Union to become all one thing or all the other—a slaveholding nation or a non-slaveholding nation—he might have said the same thing about our economic choices. Were we to remain an agrarian people, which we were before the war, or were we going to join the Industrial Revolution then afoot in the world and become an industrial giant?

The differences between the antebellum South and the antebellum North did not relate to slavery alone. In the South before the war there was little industry. In virtually every home most of the essentials of life were made from scratch—from food to clothing to implements. And most things that could not be homemade but had to be manufactured were not produced in the South. They were imported from the North or from abroad. And there was little indication this would change in their slave-dependent agrarian society.

The antebellum North was tending in an entirely different direction. On the muscle of free labor and hired help, the North was industrializing, moving from an agrarian base toward an ill-defined but heady future based on manufacturing and technology. The North was on the move toward the future, on the cusp of the Industrial Revolution which had begun in Great

Britain and was spreading planet-wide. The South was stagnating in the past.

There had been stirrings of technological development in the decade before the war, but even the North was still far more a nation of farmers working the land, an agrarian nation answering needs with its hands. The Civil War shot a tremendous jolt of creative industry through the Union that launched it finally full blown into a new economic world and put it on the road to the big city, big industry, big manufacturing, big technology, and big business society that we are today. And because the North won the war the South was obliged, with its base in slave labor destroyed, to follow whether it wished to or not. The nation was to become all one thing and not the other. It was to become a nation made in the Northern, not the Southern, image.

In the four years between April 1861 and June 1865 we learned to do something we had never done before—to mobilize, equip, arm, train, deploy, and sustain great armies. The war could not have been fought, much less won, without a tremendous industrial plant to support a huge unprecedented fighting machine and to create the weapons of destruction and the materials of war that such an effort cried for. To drive the great industrial plant needed to win the war, the North built a tremendous economic engine that would totally change our society.

The war also called urgently for a different kind of banking system—national in reach and in nature—to support this emerging behemoth and on which to erect a great industrial machine. Before the war our banking system was a balkanized operation, a grab bag of state banks. We emerged from the war with a national banking system on which our economic present has been built and on which our economic future depends.

I have often wondered what a Civil War era person, Northerner or Southerner, would think if suddenly plopped down in our twenty-first century. What would he or she think of all the things we never give a second thought to? What would they think of freeways, swarming with sleek odd looking machines racing 75 miles an hour side by side over an endless network of concrete superhighways? What would they think of subsonic and supersonic flight—huge winged machinery shooting through the air with the speed of bullets? The Civil War man or woman was not that far removed from the time when it was believed that going over 30 miles an hour would drive a human being insane. What would they think of a voice booming out of a radio, an image projected on a huge theater screen or on a small TV screen? What would they think of computers, of the Internet, that amazing web that makes communication world wide instantaneous? What would they think of elevators that can whisk them 50 stories into the sky at speeds faster than they had ever gone in their lives? What indeed would they think of the skyscrapers themselves? What would they think of air conditioning, refrigerators, and washers and dryers, and the multitude of appliances that we can't dream of living without? What would they think of the capability of mass producing anything we needed out of anything we wanted? What would they think of plastics? What indeed would they think of the magic of electricity? What would they think of this industrial world we live in? They would be astonished, indeed terrified.

They would not believe humanity, their own country, could mutate so far so fast into such a different society from theirs. Yet it happened and, to an important degree, it was all launched from their own Civil War.

REASON TWELVE
Because It Produced Men of Fabulous Fortunes

There is another kind of hero in American life—not as pure and not as sublimated as the ones who proved themselves in the smoke and fire of the Civil War and often paid for their courage with their lives.

This other variety of hero is to a degree an anti-hero, but venerated nonetheless in our society as a hero of sorts. He was the man who knew how to build a fortune and did it. We have always admired that kind of hero, the Horatio Algers among us. We have always wished to emulate them, to succeed in life as they have succeeded. For better or for worse, such skill—the ability to make and handle money on an enormous scale as adroitly as a hero-soldier handles a musket—ranks high on our scale of values. And out of the milieu of the Civil War emerged several men—three in particular—who epitomize this brand of anti-hero.

While their contemporaries went to war, these three—Andrew Carnegie, John Pierpont Morgan, and John D. Rockefeller—dodged the war and built the foundations for three of the colossal fortunes and three of the most notable careers in American business, industry, and finance. Instead of going to the battlefield like so many of their young contemporaries, they pointedly avoided that fate and instead turned their talents to doing business and beginning to build their fortunes.

There was little altruism in this at first, and a lot of backs were ruthlessly walked on by men such as these on their road to the rarefied financial realms they reached. Their shrewdness often came with a mean streak and a hard heart. However, their aims and accomplishments in the long run were not entirely self-serving. These three financial, business, and industrial wizards contributed tremendously to the economic life of the country in the decades following the war and left legacies that have immortalized them, just as the great generals of the war immortalized themselves in battle.

Of these three, Carnegie is the most hero-like in what he accomplished and how he chose to use what he accomplished for the benefit of his fellow man. He turned out not only to be a man with a phenomenal Midas touch, but one with his heart in the right place. His father was a Scotsman, a handloom weaver. His mother was the daughter of a tanner and shoemaker. They migrated with their young son—only thirteen years old—to America in 1848. And from a bobbin boy making $1.20 a week young Carnegie started his rise to the top of the industrial world. He became a crack telegrapher and soon caught on with the Pennsylvania Railroad.

When the war came he was twenty-six years old, already a young business phenomenon, head of the railroad's Western Division. He went to the war immediately in April 1861, but as a civilian—not a soldier—working in the War Office in Washington organizing railroad and telegraph communications into Virginia. His wartime service was useful—he organized the first U.S. Military Telegraphers Corps. But it was also brief. After less than six months in Washington, he returned to his job on the Pennsylvania Railroad.

Carnegie saw clearly that the industry that was being lifted to the heights by the needs of the war was the iron industry. The demand for iron was bottomless, and fortunes were being made overnight by the iron masters of Pittsburgh. Carnegie left the railroad to join the ironmasters, eventually becoming the greatest and the richest of them all. By 1873 he was into steel and soon became the nation's great steel master, with huge interests as well in bond selling, oil, bridge building, steamship lines, railroads, and other lucrative pursuits.

But always in the back of his mind was payback. In 1889 he wrote an article for the *North American Review* titled "Wealth." It was a shocker, a distillation of everything Carnegie believed about being rich—and which many other men of wealth and privilege didn't believe. It became widely known as "The Gospel of Wealth," and it held that the life of a man with the talent to make a fortune fell into two periods—the first to make the millions, the second to distribute and share them. Carnegie believed that the first obligation of a multi-millionaire—billionaires were still unknown in those times—was to see to the need of his family. But his second obligation, just as obligatory, was to spend the rest of that wealth for the public good—to hold it in trust for the benefit of his fellow man and to see it so used. He believed that the man of great wealth who didn't do this "died disgraced."

Carnegie didn't just preach this gospel, he practiced it. An avid reader, he poured money into a network of more than 2,800 Carnegie free libraries in big towns and small across the country, with "Let There Be Light" carved on every one he built. He plowed millions into churches and colleges and gave more millions for education and international peace. He died an American hero in 1919 when he was eighty-four years old—not in the end for his money, but for his good works.

J. Pierpont Morgan was twenty-four years old at the beginning of the Civil War, into foreign exchange and already on his way to the top in the business world. When the war came he simply chose not to go, and when conscription came he hired a substitute. Some of his early business moves during the war were suspect and at worst unpatriotic—early help in financing an enterprise that sold the Federal government obsolete Hall's carbines, and questionable gold speculations.

But after the war be would become an international financier unmatched in American history. In the national treasury crisis of 1895, he boldly stepped in with a syndicate that raised a $65 million gold payment that steered the country's economy out of trouble. It was widely viewed in that time as the turning point in the financial history of the decade. In 1901 Morgan was the architect of the massive merger of the big steel companies, including Carnegie's, into the United States Steel Corporation, the world giant in steel production and the first billion-dollar corporation in the world.

Like Carnegie, Morgan's interests were eclectic, his influence in the financial world gigantic, matching his commanding physique, his business acumen, his boldness, and his towering self-confidence. He was without question the foremost organizer of great business enterprises of his time, or any time. Like Carnegie he also gave back—mainly to churches, cathedrals, art museums, and hospitals. He also died an American hero of sorts. It has been said that the word "princely" was applied to him more frequently than to any other American of his time and place.

John D. Rockefeller was the youngest of the three, only twenty-one when the war came. But he clearly saw it as an opportunity to make a fortune. He had just started a produce trading company in Cleveland and was strategically placed to profit enormously from the war. He wasn't about to become a soldier. He first claimed exemption as the sole support of his mother and four younger siblings, who had been deserted by a philandering father. And, like Morgan, to avoid conscription he hired a substitute. In 1863 he plunged into an oil refining venture on which he was to build his fabulous fortune after the war. Rockefeller was ruthless in business, but he and his progeny would become noted in American life for the multi-millions they have poured into philanthropy.

These three men of enormous wealth and privilege serve in the American mind as prototypes of a kind—men with the talent to make fortunes, but who in the end understood that with great fortune comes even greater responsibility. In a sense, men such as these were anti-heroes in their time, lacking in the qualities of idealism and courage we generally associate with heroes on the battlefield. But they were formed in the same mix and in the same time frame—the Civil War—and in the end proved heroes of a kind themselves.

REASON THIRTEEN
Because It Was a War of Political Oddities

The Civil War years from 1860 to 1865 produced one of the most unique half-decade of politics in American history.

Consider these oddities:

The Democrats met in Charleston, South Carolina, in the spring of 1860 leaning toward nominating their front runner, a stubby United States senator from Illinois widely known as the "Little Giant." But when the convention tried to nominate him, the Southern delegates walked out and the crippled convention temporarily adjourned without nominating anybody.

The party tried again in Baltimore in the early summer and this time did nominate their "Little Giant." But the Southern Democrats who had walked out of the first convention didn't like him any better the second time around. They set up business down the street, proclaimed themselves the real Democratic party, and nominated an opposing ticket.

The new Republican party, barely half a decade old, meeting in convention in Chicago, also leaned heavily toward a front runner, a famous and politically seasoned New Yorker. But they ended up nominating a relatively unknown dark horse instead, a lanky Illinois lawyer-politician who thought himself so ugly that when he was accused of being two faced had said, "If I had another face do you think I would wear this one?"

A fourth party of men, despairing for the fate of the Union and not comfortable with any of the other three tickets, met and nominated a slate of their own. And the four parties, thus variously manned with their priorities and agendas, began a four-sided campaign.

The mainline Democratic candidate, the "Little Giant," trying to save the Union, went around the country, including the South, giving speeches, contrary to a political custom that frowned on presidential candidates making speeches during the campaign.

The supporters of the Republican candidate marched in the campaign in black oil-cloth slickers and carried torches and rails, the hallmark of their gangly rail-splitting candidate.

The Republican rail-splitter was elected president despite not giving a single speech, despite not receiving a single vote in the Southern states—indeed not even being on the ballot there—and despite not winning a popular majority. As soon as he was elected, seven Southern states seceded almost immediately, on no other grounds than that he had been elected.

The seven—calling themselves the Confederacy—met in Montgomery, Alabama, wrote a constitution closely patterned on the constitution of the Union they had just left, named a provisional president who didn't want to be president, and set him up in Montgomery, then in Richmond, Virginia. He was later elected to a single six-year term, beginning with his inauguration on February 22, 1862.

The Republican president-elect came to Washington to assume his duties and entered the city incognito, because his supporters feared an assassination attempt.

A month after the new president in the North was inaugurated, the new Confederate government in the South fired on Fort Sumter in Charleston harbor. The president in the North called for 75,000 volunteers to serve for ninety days to put down the rebellion. Four more border states then angrily seceded.

And so the war began and prominent politicians both North and South, without any military skill whatever, demanded to be made generals, and were, with largely predictable results.

Two years into the war the Republican president was repudiated at the polls in the mid-term elections, because he wasn't winning the war and because he had issued an edict emancipating slaves. Neither development was popular in the country.

In 1864, for the first time in history, a presidential election was held during a Civil War—but only in the North.

Most of the radical members of the president's party, wanting to be rid of him, tried to nominate somebody else in 1864. But the lanky dark horse had turned out to be one of the most acute politicians in American history, and he was renominated despite them.

For the first time in thirty years a sitting president was running for reelection. It hadn't happened since Andrew Jackson was elected to a second term in 1832. By 1864 running for reelection had fallen so out of fashion that it was considered gauche, even unthinkable.

The president, although running again, against this sentiment, wasn't sure he wanted to. But the job of winning a civil war hadn't been finished, and he didn't think it a good idea to change horses in the middle of the stream. So he ran anyhow.

One of the president's own cabinet members, his secretary of the treasury, covertly ran against his boss, even while denying he was doing it, a thing that would be unthinkable in our time.

Many Democrats, who called themselves War Democrats, had become Republicans for the duration of the war, in the interest of putting down the rebellion. Many of them found the association rather strained and unnatural but did it anyhow.

The Republicans, to attract and pacify such Democratic deviants, didn't call themselves the Republican Party anymore but the National Union Party.

The candidate for that part of the Democratic Party still faithful to its name was a popular general whom the incumbent president had sacked two years before for failing to fight hard enough.

This Democratic standard bearer, being a military man, hated politicians and politics in general but ran anyhow on a platform plank that he roundly repudiated, which said the war he had helped wage for two years was a failure.

It was a time when editors not only wrote editorials, but were major political players. The editor of the *New York Times* was the Republican national chairman running the president's campaign. The editor of the *New York World* was a member of the Democratic candidate's brain trust, and the editor of the *New York Tribune* was a Republican stump speaker.

The Confederates, though not directly involved, believed, like many members of the Northern president's own party, that in their interests he must be defeated. They sent agents into Canada with a million dollars to try to buy or influence the election in favor of the Democratic general who they believed would be more sympathetic to peace and Southern independence.

As the election neared, the war was not going well for the North and the Republican president became convinced he could not win a second term. So he wrote a sealed note pledging that after he lost he would work with the new Democratic president-elect to end the war before the inauguration on March 4, 1865.

But one of the president's admirals won a great naval victory in Mobile Bay on August 5, one of his generals captured Atlanta on September 2, and another of his generals beat the

Confederates in the Shenandoah Valley on September 19 and then routed them in the same valley four weeks later.

So the president, with these telling stump speeches from his admiral and two generals, won the election despite himself, despite the discontents in his own party, despite the Democrats, and despite the Confederates.

Again the president made not a speech in his own behalf in the campaign and the Democratic candidate was even less visible, making only three public appearances in the campaign and not speaking at any of them.

Some of the campaign tactics on both sides, violating every shade of conflicting interest, would have caused a Watergate-sized scandal today, but caused only a slight ripple then. It was the way politics was practiced.

The soldiers in the army, many of them voting in the field for the first time, voted heavily against the general who had been one of their most popular commanders, indeed one of the most popular in American military history.

The defeated general vowed never to have anything to do with politics again, and several years later was elected governor of New Jersey.

In the spring of 1865, little more than a month after he was inaugurated for a second term and after Robert E. Lee had surrendered to U.S. Grant at Appomattox Courthouse, the president who had seen the war successfully won was assassinated, the first chief executive in our history to be slain in office. He would not be the last.

And so it went in the political world during that incredible window in time called the Civil War. It was politics as usual in that time, but viewed a century and a half later it was politics that was odd and incredible and worth anybody's study, then or now.

REASON FOURTEEN
Because It Pioneered a New Journalism

The surge in inventiveness that the Civil War unleashed flushed out an army of legitimate and not so legitimate inventors with odd and not so odd inventions with which to wage war.

One of these new devices was a repeating gun that prevented the escape of gas. Abraham Lincoln went to look at it, as he often did with new inventions, and was impressed. "Well," he said, after inspecting it, "I believe this really does what it is represented to do. Now have any of you heard of any machine, or invention, for preventing the escape of 'gas' from newspaper establishments?"

It was not necessarily a laughing matter, this escape of gas from newspaper establishments. Newspapers in the nineteenth century were powerful opinion makers and objectivity was not generally their cardinal tenet. They routinely mixed their colors from the palette of their particular political prejudices. The editors were major players in their times, sounding off in the idiom of their biases in whatever was going on, inserting themselves and their newspapers, their opinions and their gratuitous advice, into the middle of affairs, damning what they didn't like, extolling what they did like, irrespective of the facts in the case. The reporting, such as it was, was heavily tinted with the particular newspaper's political point of view. Injecting that point of view not only into editorials but into what passed as news stories was what editors believed their mission in life to be and what newspapers were for.

After Lincoln delivered his Gettysburg address in November 1863, the pro-Lincoln Republican newspapers, following their pro-Lincoln biases, generally hailed it as the masterpiece it was. But the Democratic papers, following their anti-Lincoln biases, damned and derided it. One Democratic paper reported that the president had once again made an ass of himself.

But just as the Civil War forced new thinking in many things, it forced new thinking in journalism. The war was the biggest news event of the mid-nineteenth century in America. It demanded more than editorial opinion—that leaking of gas, which not even the most inventive minds knew how to stop. It also demanded to be covered. And there was an editor in New York who saw that more clearly than most. And that he saw it is perhaps ironic, because he was cross-eyed.

James Gordon Bennett, editor of the *New York Herald*, was so terribly cross-eyed, one who knew him said, "that when he looked at me with one eye, he looked out at the City Hall with the other." And when his journalistic and political enemies ridiculed him for this defect, he snapped back that it stemmed from trying to follow their political movements.

But as an editor who seemed to sense what readers wanted to read, Bennett was straight-sighted. Even before the war he had been dishing out not just editorial opinion and insult—which he dished out with the best—but with it a genuine reporting of events. It was not necessarily unvarnished reporting. But it was reporting. Bennett founded the *Herald* on $500 in a New York basement in 1835—"one poor man," as he put it, "in a cellar against the world." In the antebellum years he had turned his newspaper into the most readable, popular, and sensational in the country. The slashing editorial opinions in the paper were mortared with solid reporting of breaking events. He soon had his paper doing things no other paper was doing—reporting news. The *Herald* was the first general-interest newspaper to cover sports, business, stocks, and crime—in all its sensational and lurid details.

When the war came, Bennett recognized it for what it was, the most sensational news story of the nineteenth century, and sent a stable of well-paid correspondents to cover it and report what they saw. The other major New York papers, despite their distaste for Bennett, whom they considered unscrupulous and called "Old Satanic," had to do likewise. And a new age of reportorial journalism was born.

Not only did newspapers send reporters to the battlefield, but also artists with pencils and sketch pads and a pictorial eye, doing then what the still cameras and TV cameras do in such profusion and merciless detail today. Photography was not sufficiently developed in the Civil War years to picture war as it happened. But a handful of pioneering photographers, chief among them Mathew Brady, appeared on the major battlefields of the war within hours or days after the firing stopped to set up their bulky equipment and to capture the resulting carnage on film. It was the first war ever to be covered extensively by photojournalists. The still pictures they shot give us the dramatic images that today are seared into our memories and, indeed, epitomize the war to many of us—ghastly pictures of wasted soldiers lying still, stiff, bloated, and dead on a shot-torn battlefield.

The reporters and artists and photographers of the Civil War were the forerunners of the ubiquitous print and TV war correspondents we know today. Subsequent wars have brought us armies of them, improving their craft with each war and with each technological advance, reporting battle with an ever more practiced, sharp, dramatic, and accurate eye. In World War II a handful of journalists became household names, immortalized because they so expertly and movingly reported what they saw. It was a war that produced Ernie Pyle and Edward R. Morrow and Bill Mauldin.

War reporting since their time has been taken to yet another level, most recently in the Gulf War in 1991 with the sensational on-the-scene TV coverage exemplified by CNN reporters, and then in the Iraqi war of 2003. In the invasion of Iraq we got for the first time the "embedded reporter," news men and women folded into fighting units on the field, basically becoming soldiers themselves, embedded there to report what they saw. They were the heirs of the legendary combat correspondents of World War II

The germ of all that now comprises the modern day you-are-there, in-your-face style of journalism was incubated in the Civil War. The correspondents and artists sent out by the editor-generals of that war became the harbingers of what we have today—all encompassing, often over-surfeited coverage that dissects every part of every day of a war, in up close, personal, and often numbing detail.

REASON FIFTEEN
Because It Inspired Great Literature

One of the giants of American literature in the nineteenth century occupied the White House in the Civil War.

Historians in a sense are still trying to figure out Abraham Lincoln. Few men in history have been written about so much. Perhaps none soared into the American consciousness with such unexpected suddenness, from such an unexpected and unpromising beginning, and filled it with such power, purpose, and presence. Few in our history equal this unlettered, self-taught man as a lawyer, politician, and statesman. In any listing by historians of the best of our presidents, Lincoln is generally topmost, surpassing even Washington.

And in any listing of giants of American literature, he is also there. Lincoln was a great writer and to some degree he set the standard for the body of great writing that flowed and continues to flow from that national experience known as the American Civil War.

When I was speaking to a class of university students some time ago, one of them asked me if Lincoln came back to life and I could ask him one question, what would it be. As a writer, I hardly thought twice about it. I would ask him how he wrote so well. How did that man, with less than a year's formal education, become such a master of the written word?

Lord George Nathaniel Curzon, the British statesman and man of letters after Lincoln's time, spoke of what he believed to be the three greatest orations in the English language. Two of the three, Curzon believed, were by Lincoln—the Gettysburg Address and the Second Inaugural. The third was the toast of British Prime Minister William Pitt after the British naval victory over the French and Spanish fleets in 1805.

Lincoln wrote as he acted, to the necessity of the times. In such a national crisis it is critical that the voice coming from the highest echelon of national life speak with force and clarity. Lincoln wrote and spoke with brilliant force and clarity. One need only read his words to understand he is in the presence of a master writer.

The Civil War, as unbeautiful as it was, has left us a beautiful legacy of words. As Lincoln was writing to the necessity of the times, so were many others, on both sides of the war, of both genders, of all ages and persuasions and social strata. This greatest event of America's nineteenth century demanded that those fighting in it, living through it, say something about it. It cried for people to write what they were seeing, feeling, and experiencing—to give voice, to articulate their deepest emotions, if only for themselves.

Many Northerners and Southerners kept diaries and journals—or later wrote vivid memoirs of the war. Virginia Davis Gray, beginning a diary in Arkansas, wrote:

"By the parlor fire, one Saturday night
We sat to write our journal
Expecting to write by the bright pine light
The events of the past diurnal.
'O give me paper,' Roberta cries
'That I a journal may keep
And see with my eyes how fast time flies
Before I lie down to sleep.'"

Many simply wrote letters. An ocean of correspondence, some of it brilliantly written, was put on paper in the Civil War. Hundreds of these diaries, journals, and memoirs, thousands of these letters, have been preserved in archives or published, making the Civil War one of the most poignantly and personally documented passages in world history. With no planning, simply by reflex action, the Civil War created great literature on a gut level.

In the act of writing a book, *Surviving the Confederacy*, I combed scores of women's journals and diaries. It was a moving experience to read such writing, written with such style, of such sorrow and exhilaration, in such an anguished time. Twentieth century Americans, many of whom had never read anything about the war, got a heady taste of the power and eloquence of Civil War writing from the heart in Ken Burns's moving documentary film about the war that aired on National Public Television in 1990. Who was not moved, watching that series, by the eloquence of Sullivan Ballou, the doomed major of the Second Rhode Island Volunteers, writing home to his wife Sarah on the eve of the Battle of Bull Run, in which he would die:

He wrote:

"Sarah my love for you is deathless. It seems to bind me with mighty cables that nothing but Omnipotence could break. And yet my love of country comes over me like a strong wind and bears me irresistibly, with all these chains, to the battlefield.

"The memory of all the blissful moments I have enjoyed with you come crowding over me, and I feel most deeply grateful to God and you that I have enjoyed them so long. And how hard it is for me to give them up and burn to ashes the hopes of future years when, God willing, we might still have lived and loved together and seen our sons grow up to honorable manhood around us. . . .

"If I do not return, my dear Sarah, never forget how much I love you, nor that when my last breath escapes me on the battlefield, it will whisper your name. Forgive my many faults and the many pains I have caused you. How thoughtless, how foolish I have sometimes been.

"But, oh Sarah! If the dead can come back to this earth and flit unseen around those they love, I shall always be with you in the brightest days and in the darkest nights. Always. Always.

"And when the soft breeze fans your cheek, it shall be my breath; and as the cool air fans your throbbing temple, it shall be my spirit passing by. Sarah, do not mourn me dead: Think I am gone and wait for me, for we shall meet again."

Such writing from the soul and from the heart, moves the human heart as little else can. And much of such eloquence originated on battlefields and around hearthsides in the crucible of the Civil War. Its power is in its truth. Its emotion-stirring power comes from the truth of the living moment. That is perhaps why the literature of fact, rather than the literature of fiction, speaks most powerfully to us from the Civil War era.

I have never read a work of Civil War fiction, written then or after, that is as moving, as powerful, as poignant as what really happened. The Civil War as it happened is tough to top for unvarnished truth and drama. There has been some compelling and popular fiction written about the war since the war, Stephen Crane's *Red Badge of Courage*, Margaret Mitchell"s' *Gone with the Wind*, Michael Shaara's *The Killer Angels*. But for the most significant and moving literature of the war, one must read what was written in the crucible of the war itself from the pens and hearts of those living it. It constitutes a unique legacy.

And the beat goes on. Literally hundreds of books about the war are being written and published annually. Entire generations of historians and writers have attempted and are still attempting to capture and recapture its essence and its drama and its fascination. Some of this writing has been good, some banal or worse. But some of it has attained the rarefied level of literature. Some of the best historical writing of any time and place has been by historians and writers writing about the Civil War: Bruce Catton's works, Shelby Foote's brilliant three-volume history, Alan Nevins's epic eight-volumes on the war for the Union, the biographical imagery of Douglas Southall Freeman on Lee and Carl Sandburg on Lincoln, the histories and biographies and studies by such modern day historians as James M. McPherson, David Donald, James I. Robertson, William C. Davis, and Grady McWhiney.

These retellings and relivings of the war continue to draw us dramatically back to it. The output is legion. The war has left us a body of literature unmatched in any era of history. And it continues to grow and to draw and to fascinate us again and again.

REASON SIXTEEN
Because It Tested Our Faith

While most Americans North and South chose up sides in the Civil War, it is not at all clear that Providence did.

Of all the institutions caught in the middle in the Civil War few were more unnaturally stressed than religion. The United States in 1861 was one of the world's leading Christian nations, all North and South believing in the one and only identically same God. And when the split came and states seceded, none could claim to take God with them, although most believed they must have Him on their side if they were going to win. It was a war that would test everybody's faith and, for some, shake it to the core.

Abraham Lincoln, again, had a clear grasp of the situation. In his Second Inaugural Address in March 1865, he said of the two sides in the war: "Both read the same Bible, and pray to the same God; and each invokes His aid against the other. . . . The prayers of both could not be answered; that of neither has been answered fully. The Almighty has His own purposes."

It was very difficult to put a finger on what God's purposes were in the war, if indeed He had any. It was open to interpretation and dispute from beginning to end. Lincoln was perhaps being more realistic than most when he said that it would be nice to have God on his side, but that having Kentucky might be a good deal more necessary.

As with almost everything else, God's will was often seen through the prism of one's sectional bias. It was clear to many, and often announced by ministers of the gospel, that God was on their side in the war because their cause was the righteous one. But it is clear in hindsight that nobody—no preacher, no man of the cloth, no layman—had a grip on just what God's purpose was in the war. All assumed that He was aware of what was going on, but nobody had clear proof that was the case either. All liked to believe God was working his purpose out and that He was bound to come down on their side, it being the righteous side. And when a battle was won, it was often pointed to by the victor as proof that God was indeed with them all the way and that because of it ultimate victory was certain. But that was a shaky assumption at best, often disproved by defeat in the next big battle. When that next battle was lost, there was a lot of explaining that had to be done. And no explanation was ever completely satisfactory.

It became common ecclesiastical wisdom to measure success or failure in battle against the wrath or benevolence of the Almighty, to assume that defeat meant you didn't have things straight with God, that there were some sins that had to be corrected to get things back on track. Get right with God and victory would then follow. But this was also a questionable assumption. And when the South finally lost the war, it indicated to many Southerners that some very large sins had to be rectified, that perhaps the biggest of all, indeed, had been slavery itself.

What was clear was the fact that both sides were banking on some help from the same Almighty, personally and as nations. Soldiers facing death on the battlefield needed something bigger than themselves to hang on to and to believe in—some greater power to preserve their lives. That often didn't work either. But it made it easier to die believing God controlled man's destiny and guided his fate.

No man in the war believed this stronger than "Stonewall" Jackson. An ardent Presbyterian, Jackson saw God's hand in every one of his victories, and invariably gave Providence the full credit in each. Jackson didn't live long enough to experience a major defeat. So it was not clear what he would have thought of that. However, when it came time to die in 1863 he was content, believing it was God's will, and being God's will it was the absolutely right thing to be happening. When he said in his last breath that he must cross the river and rest in the shade of the trees, he knew it was in obedience to Providence working His purpose out in his death as well as in his life.

It was that kind of faith that sustained many in the war. It is a faith that sustains most of us still. But if the war teaches us anything, it is that we can't necessarily count on God's being on our side when we choose up sides and begin fighting one another.

REASON SEVENTEEN
Because It Is Our Own Direct Tie to the Past

Lewis Carroll's Alice passed through the looking glass into a world of her imagination. For thousands of Americans the Civil War has been the looking glass through which they have journeyed into their own personal past.

The genealogy craze that has gripped the country in recent times owes much to the Civil War. It has become the main foyer over which many of us have passed to discover where we came from and who we are. The Civil War was such an exclusively American experience—and our ties to those who fought in it or lived through are but a few short generations in the past. It is perhaps not too much to say that nearly all of us have ancestry or personal interests, direct or indirect, dating back to that time. Our great-grandfathers and great-great-grandfathers fought in it. Our great-grandmothers and great-great-grandmothers lived through it.

Rarely has there been an experience in the past that so directly relates to so many of us in such a personal way. It has taken on more of a life than the typical distant event in the past. The knowledge that a direct ancestor experienced such a monumental event in history has driven the past home to us as nothing else can. It often takes such immediacy to convince us of history's abiding relevance to us in our own time.

A high school classmate recently sent me a memoir written by her great-grandmother of her experiences as a young girl in the Civil War. There is a pride in such connection and a gee-whiz kind of immediacy to it. Suddenly the Civil War, an immediate experience in the life of her great-grandmother, has become an immediate experience in her own life nearly a century and a half later, a connection to the past that has made that past come alive for her as nothing else could.

History often appears as something so distant, so alien to our present, that it excites little interest. The drama of the past alone makes it compelling to many of us, but history too often is a turn-off to many people. The dates, the droning recitation of dry fact, stripped of the human drama that drove it so long ago, has not endeared it to the masses.

The Civil War, in linking us directly to that past, has in part restored its great drama to our lives. And it is a past that is so accessible to us. It can be returned in an instant. The thousands who have traced their Civil War ancestors have learned that it is not all that difficult. Genealogical collections and libraries abound. Our past lies in the hundreds of city and county records around the country, and in the thousands of cemeteries where so many of us have gone and found where the stories ended. The TV programs, the hundreds of books coming out, readily feed this desire to know and understand our past because we want to know and understand our own relation to it. And in learning about our ancestors in the Civil War we learn about ourselves, things about us we might not otherwise ever know.

Sometimes it is information we just as soon didn't know. We might have had a criminal or a coward or a deserter in the family. Somebody in our line might have been hanged. But we might just as easily have had a hero or a martyr in our line—

more likely than not. And if our family hero was not a great-great-grandfather-soldier on the battlefield it was a great-great-grandmother left at home whose courage matched her soldier husband's and whose love sustained him. Often that was the greatest courage of all.

In researching *Surviving the Confederacy*, the thing that struck me with such force was the similarity between our ancestors of Civil War times and us, between their love and our love, their passion and our passion. Our great-great-grandmothers and grandfathers suffered the same sorrows, thrilled to the same events, thought the same thoughts, loved just as hard and just as dearly as their great-great-granddaughters and grandsons do today. To understand their feelings and emotions is to understand better our own, just as to know them helps us know ourselves.

Abraham Lincoln's favorite verse, which he quoted often for the truth it so clearly caught, was "Oh! Why Should the Spirit of Mortal Be Proud?" by William Knox. In part it went this way:

"Oh! why should the spirit of mortal be proud?
Like a swift-fleeting meteor, a fast-flying cloud,
A flash of the lightning, a break of the wave,
Man passeth from life to his rest in the grave. . . .

"For we are the same our fathers have been;
We see the same sights our fathers have seen;
We drink the same stream, and view the same sun,
And run the same course our fathers have run.

"The thoughts we are thinking our fathers would think;
From the death we are shrinking our fathers would shrink;
To the life we are clinging they also would cling;
But it speeds for us all, like a bird on the wing. . . .

"They died, aye! they died; and we things that are now,
Who walk on the turf that lies over their brow,
Who make in their dwelling a transient abode,
Meet the things that they met on their pilgrimage road. . . .

"'Tis the wink of an eye, 'tis the draught of a breath,
From the blossom of health to the paleness of death,
From the gilded saloon to the bier and the shroud—
Oh! why should the spirit of mortal be proud?"

Our kinship with the past is tight and inseparable. The Civil War lives yet in our genes.

REASON EIGHTEEN
Because It Makes Us Remember

Reunion is an important word in the American experience. Reunion was what the Civil War was all about.

And today reunions are a big part of who we are. We have family and high school and college reunions, and military reunions. They are a mechanism by which we remember, recall, and relive times in our lives that we don't want to forget, things that are such a vital part of who we were and who we are. James Russell Lowell, the nineteenth century American man of letters, wrote that old events have modern meanings, that only that which finds kindred in all hearts and lives survives. That is what in our past survives and drives us ultimately back to that past, reuniting us with it once again, and over and over again.

We are a nation that puts a high value on nostalgia and reliving our earlier years. Our roots, like the tap roots of trees, are such a part of us. And if our past had joy, as so much of our past does, the compulsion to revisit it and relive it is compelling. Some years ago when my high school class from Tucson Senior High in Arizona had its twenty-fifth reunion, I went. It was the first time in a quarter century that I had seen many of those young men and women from my past, and I had no idea what to expect. But when I got there, among such familiar old and beloved names and faces—somewhat altered from our younger years, I admit—it was a warm reuniting with my past. We all picked up where we left off. The twenty-five years that separated most of us melted away in an instant of recognition and recollection. It was a highlight experience in my life, just as the high school experience itself had been. That high school class has held reunions at least every five years since and I have returned for all of them with the joy of anticipation and rekindled affections. I have found them to be not simply a reunion of old friends, but a reunion of hearts. And the older I get the more precious these reunitings are because they express the abiding love we had and still have for one another.

I look on history as reunion on a large canvass—a going back to our tap root, invoking our memories on a city, county, state, nation, world, and universal scale. It has been said that with the loss of tradition, we lose the thread that has guided us through "the vast realms of the past." In reunion that thread is sustained, linking succeeding generations with past generations, us with those who went before.

History has been defined by many great minds in many different ways in many different ages. Henry Ford, that genius American industrialist and irascible disciple of his time, reportedly said history is bunk (although he insisted he was misquoted). Along the same train of thought Carl Sandburg, the American poet and biographer of Lincoln, called history "a bucket of ashes." Voltaire, the eighteenth century French philosopher and author, thought history a pack of tricks we play upon the dead. The English playwright and novelist, Oscar Wilde, said history is merely gossip. Agreeing with him, that American iconoclast of the nineteenth century, Ambrose Bierce, defined a historian as "a broad-gauged gossip." For Patrick Henry, that great American patriot of the Revolution, history was a compass. He said, "I know of no other way of judging the future but by the past." And Robert E. Lee said it is history that teaches us to hope.

I like best what Winston Churchill, the great British prime minister and historian, said of history. "History," Churchill wrote, "stumbles along the trail of the past, trying to reconstruct its scenes, to revive its echoes, and kindle with pale gleams the passion of former days."

To stumble along the trail of our Civil War past, reconstructing its scenes, reviving its echoes, rekindling with pale gleams its enormous passions, is what I now do in the twilight years of my own life. I am in constant reunion with that epic passage in the American past. Every day I go back to it and every day I am enriched by it. My wife never knows if I will be home again in this century in time for dinner

The study of that war makes us remember something we must never forget—how it was we came to a crisis of such enormous moment in our history and lived and fought through it and came out in the end not only preserved as a unique democratic republic, but made better by it.

REASON NINETEEN
Because It is Great Drama

Many people decry history. All of us know people who said they hated it in school. It was their least favorite subject. They saw it as what that twentieth century Russian revolutionary, Leon Trotsky, said it was—a "dustbin"—full of rancid and dull facts, names, battles, places, wars, treaties, acts, and dates nobody wanted to recall, an incomprehensible jumble of useless disjointed information marching along in pointless lock step and having to be memorized.

That misses the entire point of history. And there is only one reason it is viewed that way by many, only one reason everybody doesn't love history in school and continues to love it throughout their lives: It wasn't taught right. When it is taught correctly and with passion, it is everybody's favorite subject.

There are two basic kinds of history—studies, which academic historians mainly deal in, and stories, which the writers and teachers of narrative history tell. And history as a story is great drama. Viewing it as a series of dramatic scenes involving people, you can travel back in time and set down anywhere in any age and something fascinating and dramatic is happening. Somebody is doing something utterly riveting, and probably doing it to somebody else. History, taught and written as drama in all of its nuances, is irresistible, more engaging than any book of fiction ever written. Edward Bellamy, the nineteenth century American author, wrote that "on no other stage are the scenes shifted with a swiftness so like magic as on the great stage of history when once the hour strikes."

History is a fantastic story about people. It has every element of dramatic fiction. It has tension and conflict. It has plot and subplot and counterplot. It has drama. It casts lights and shadows into all the corners of human conduct. It is a page turner, and what makes it better than fiction is the fact that it is fact—it is true. It really happened.

Willa Cather, the twentieth century American novelist, said that the history of every country begins in the heart of a man or a woman. That is indeed what history is all about. It is what the Civil War boils down to. It is a story that begins—and ends—in the hearts of those who lived it. And passing it down the ages is akin to what Sara Pryor, a Confederate woman writing after the Civil War, said of passing one thought from heart to heart—it is like passing "a bit of flame" from one age to another.

If somebody detested history in school it was because it was not taught as a great story, as drama—as a bit of flame—passing from heart to heart. The late Stephen Ambrose, who wrote history with verve and insight, bringing it vividly to life, said once in an interview: "Academic history has lost the power of the narrative. It's lost its audience. And they don't even know it. Their audience is the eighteen, nineteen-year-old American. And those kids come into the classroom and look up at you and say, 'Tell us about our heroes and what did they do?' And they don't get any answer from academic historians. And as a consequence the kids don't take history courses. And as a consequence of that, history departments go down in size. And the aggrieved professors never figure out why."

Ambrose, an academic historian who did figure out why, tried to tell the others, "Look, you got to tell them about George Washington and Thomas Jefferson [or in Ambrose's case about

Lewis and Clark or the hero-soldiers of World War II] then, after that, you can get into the role of women, demographic statistics and stuff like that. But you got to tell them what it was really like at Valley Forge. And how tough Washington's decision was in dealing with the Hessians. You have to give them the foundation of what this country's all about."

What history is all about is people. What Ambrose said of George Washington and Thomas Jefferson must also be said of the heroes of the Civil War. History that grips the imagination is the history that tells about people and what happened to them in their particular moment in history—history told as a whopping good story.

When you read about the Civil War, read about the people in it. A wonderful way to read history, indeed, is simply to read biographies. Read of Lincoln and Davis, Lee and Grant, and Jackson and Sherman. Read of Clara Barton and Frederick Douglass. Anybody who reads of the Civil War—reads all history—as the great human drama that it was, never tires of reading it.

REASON Twenty
Because It Speaks to Us Still

The Civil War still continues to stir the American imagination—more than anything ever has—bulking larger in our minds than any single event in our history.

It was uniquely "our war." And In these times its memory is stirred and restirred constantly. No event in our past has evoked such an outpouring of telling and retelling. The books about it and about those who fought and led it have become virtually uncountable and are still pouring from presses in a tidal wave of words. Its most spectacular leap into our present-day imagination was triggered by Ken Burns's eleven-part documentary, which has been run and rerun so often since. That long look back, using the magic of television, injected the war into the national psyche again as nothing ever had, bringing it dramatically back to us as large as life. More than any one thing it helped spawn the enormous and growing subculture of the Civil War that has sent thousands of Americans reading, thousands more to the preserved battlefields of the war, and other thousands to reenactments of the battles they have read about.

Many of those same readers and tourists and reenactors, and others hungering to learn of their blood kinship to the Civil War, are flocking to genealogical archives across the country in search of their own histories. Today the subculture is populated by a vast network of Civil War Round Tables, Sons of Confederate Veterans, Sons of Union Veterans, and United

Daughters of the Confederacy camps, and organizations dedicated to preserving the battlefields of our Civil War past. Many gifted Civil War historians have become superstars in their own right because of their knowledge of the war and their talents in teaching or writing of it, or their unique ability to lead busloads of tourists to where the fighting happened and make it spring to life once more.

The Civil War has never been so accessible as it is today. Fought as it was on American soil, its traces and its remnants are everywhere. National Battlefield Parks are magnets for the American people. And although much land where battles were fought has been plowed under by advancing development, much has been saved. And the battle to save what is left and endangered is being masterfully waged by the Civil War Preservation Trust and its allies. Artifacts of the war abound, and more appear every day to be bought by eager collectors.

For a time I lived on sixteen acres of ground at the foot of Rich Mountain in West Virginia, on the old Staunton-Parkersburg Pike that snaked over the Appalachian and Allegheny ranges from Virginia to the Ohio River. The pike hadn't changed in its twists and turns over Rich Mountain since before the Civil War. The same rutted dirt surface that was there in July 1861 when one of the first engagements of the war was fought on its summit still existed, wending past my front door. On the eastern edge of my property was the remnant of Confederate Camp Garnett, dug in there to keep the Union forces of George McClellan from passing through and over the mountain into Beverly. Remnants of the Confederate trenches still show dimly on the face of the land. My house stood not far from where McClellan must have nervously surveyed the situation through his binoculars. Two miles above the Confederate encampment, on the top of the mountain, the battle was fought on July 11 following a day-long arduous Federal flanking move-ment. The Confederates were defeated, the old Confederate encampment on my land, caught between two Union forces, was abandoned and Beverly occupied by Union soldiers.

Often in the still of the night my vivid imagination fancied it heard the tread of marching feet and the roll of caissons. It was only my imagination, of course. But that is the way the Civil War is. It stirs the imagination and quickens expectations and does it to this day. It is vivid in our memories because it is still so vivid to our sight.

The Civil War is such a vibrant part of the tapestry of our past, yet it lives so vividly still in the present, that to know our-selves we must know it. So many aspects of our lives took root in some way in that unique and stormy passage in our history. That is reason enough in its own right, powerful enough, to drive our memories indefinitely back to it, as doubtless it always will as long as we exist as a people and a nation.

How to Study It

There is no one way to enter the world of the Civil War, no one looking-glass into Wonderland, no one magic wardrobe into Narnia. It can be entered in many different ways.

Television and the Internet notwithstanding, the greatest magic carpet ride for the mind ever devised by man is books. And that is still the best way to enter and understand the past, still the best route to relive its drama. However, the first two can't be discounted, nor should they be. History on television can be made very moving and very dramatic, which is how history ought to be perceived. Ken Burns, the History Channel, and other documentary and feature filmmakers have shown that in recent times. The Internet daily is becoming a more rich and reliable window through which to enter the past. And if you want to make your journey through the Civil War website by website, there is an excellent guide to help you through that bewildering labyrinth past the many shoals and rapids of inaccurate information—*The Civil War on the Web: A Guide to the Very Best Sites*, by Alice E. Carter and Richard Jensen.

Yet another route many are taking to plug into the drama of the Civil War is history tours, led by expert historians such as Edwin Cole Bearss, a charismatic walking Civil War encyclopedia preternaturally gifted in vividly reviving that drama for busloads of history lovers. The Smithsonian Institution has long offered a popular schedule of Civil War tours around Washington. HistoryAmerica TOURS, a leading history tour company, annually offers a stimulating repertoire of tours and cruises into the American past.

But no matter how many TV programs you watch, no matter how many websites you visit, no matter how many tours you take, you will still eventually have to ride that ultimate magic carpet, the book, to fully and deeply savor the Civil War. It was the looking glass and wardrobe through which I entered. It is still the preeminent gateway, leading up the most satisfying pathway.

The Civil War can be approached and embraced broadly—taking it all on at once and in whole, before breaking it down and attacking it piece by piece. Or it can be entered in the opposite way, by taking one piece, one battle, one event, one man or woman, for study, specializing at first in that and then branching out from there into the Civil War's wider world. Both approaches are entirely satisfactory and satisfying in their own ways.

The sources I will mention here are by no means or in any way comprehensive. They are simply a brief, very brief, compilation of some of the books about the Civil War that have inspired me personally.

I began by first consuming the whole loaf. I started with the magisterial eight-volume work on the war and the conflict leading up to it by Alan Nevins. Those eight volumes, spread over three parts—*The Ordeal of the Union, The Emergence of Lincoln,* and The *War for the Union* —constitute a sweeping masterwork of narrative history that takes the reader down the road to disunion and through the war itself. It is breathtakingly comprehensive, anecdote-rich, and eminently readable. It made me hunger for more. After reading it, I threw myself immediately into yet another sweeping whole-loaf account, Bruce Catton's classic three-volume *The Centennial History of the Civil War,* a work that shows how history can also be great literature. Not through with taking the war in whole, I next immersed myself in yet another sweeping classic masterpiece of narrative history, Shelby Foote's magnificent three-volume *The Civil War: A Narrative.*

However, the full loaf doesn't necessarily have to come in multiple volumes to be outstanding. There are good, reliable one-volume accounts of the entire war as well. And the one that stands out above all others is James M. McPherson's *Battle Cry of Freedom: The Civil War Era,* a compelling, accurate, dramatic, highly readable account by one of the greatest of Civil War historians.

For a tantalizing and fact-satisfying taste of virtually every conceivable aspect of the Civil War in one massive volume, there is now available the marvelous, comprehensive, new, and highly readable *Encyclopedia of the American Civil War: A Political, Social, and Military History,* edited by David S. Heidler and Jeanne T. Heidler, published in 2000.

Reading the epic stories of the two great armies of the East— the Union Army of the Potomac and the Confederate Army of Northern Virginia— is yet another way to cut a broad opening swath through the Civil War. A stimulating, highly readable way to do that for the Union army is with Bruce Catton's three-volume work on the Army of the Potomac: *Mr. Lincoln's Army, Glory Road,* and *A Stillness at Appomattox.* The Army of Northern Virginia has been covered in detail in an equal number of volumes with equal skill by Douglas Southall Freeman in *Lee's Lieutenants: A Study in Command.* These are both masterworks of Civil War history by master craftsmen.

Those broad-gauged narratives, taken together or separately, constitute an excellent comprehensive full-frontal approach to the sweep of the Civil War. They will lead you on and on down multiple endless pathways, rich in scenic detail, teeming with fascinating characters, redolent in feeling and atmosphere. What to read next depends on where your interests take you. These initial readings will suggest good follow-up reading in every direction. And as you go down the road of your particular choice, one book will lead to another. That is the way it works. And the only limit to the riches you will find is your own will to continue in whatever direction you have chosen. When one direction is satisfied, other pathways can be likewise taken and explored to the limits of your individual interest.

There are also books about books about the Civil War, excellent bibliographical studies and listings. One of the first, best, and most comprehensive bibliographies—including an exhaustive list of the best biographies of all the notable figures in the war—is in James G. Randall's and David Donald's The *Civil War and Reconstruction,* published in 1969. There have since been several comprehensive bibliographical studies of the war, notably and most recently *The Civil War in Books: An Analytical Bibliography,* by David J. Eicher, and *Writing the Civil War: A Quest to Understand,* by James M. McPherson and William J. Cooper, Jr.

All of these books I've mentioned so far are secondary sources, books written or compiled by historians and writers who did not witness the events they are writing about or live in the time they happened. To study the Civil War in ultimate detail up close and personal, you have to do what those historians and writers have had to do—go to the primary sources, those written or compiled by the actors in the great drama itself or by those who lived while the drama was playing out on the national stage. These are the first-hand records of the time, locked in reports, accounts, newspapers, magazines, diaries, memoirs, and letters written in the time or later by the people of the time. The Civil War was, as I have noted, an event so staggering, so calamitous, so unique that people who lived then were driven, almost compelled, to record it in some way through their own eyes and their own passions. Many such sources abound. On them is based the torrent of books that have since been written and continue to be written about the Civil War.

There exist several outstanding published multi-volume compilations of records and writings by the actors and observers of the drama. Foremost of those is the massive 128-volume *War of the Rebellion: A Compilation of the Official Records of the Union and Confederate Armies.* Before I began writing books about the Civil War, this was the first set of primary sources I ever purchased (understandably over time). Another rich and rewarding must-consult source is *Battles and Leaders of the Civil War,* a compilation of first hand accounts and interpretations written by major surviving players in the war, North and South. It was first published as a series of articles in *The Century Magazine,* then edited into four volumes by Robert Underwood Johnson and Clarence Clough Buel and available today in reprint editions.

Equally rich in documenting the full sweep of the war in a very personal way are various sets of multiple-volume first-hand accounts on both the Union and Confederate sides. The most comprehensive and variety-rich published collections of Union accounts are the *Military Order of the Loyal Legion of the United States; The Papers of the Military Historical Society of Massachusetts;* and *The Rebellion Record: A Diary of American Events.* Equally rich on the Confederate side are The *Confederate Veteran,* bound issues of the Confederate Veteran Magazine collected and published by the National Historical Society; the bound volumes of *The Southern Historical Society Papers;* and the multi-volume *Confederate Military History*, covering separately each of the Confederate states in the war.

These volumes are not all easy to find or to own. I own them all because I am a junkie and a writer and my wife is very understanding of my passions. I constantly go back to them over and over in my own journey to study, understand, and write of the war. All of them are available in a good university library.

That in a sketchy, scratch-the-surface way, is my own personal take on how to begin the journey by first swallowing the whole in the manner that I did. The other approach, just as valid, is to begin with a single event in the war, a battle or otherwise, or a figure in it, which, for one reason or another fascinates you. Think of it, or of him and her, and there is very likely a book, often many books, that cover the subject—in detail. And yet another perhaps about to come out.

Virtually every battle in the war has been refought detail-by-detail at least once between covers. The books about major landmarks, war-turning battles such as Gettysburg, can cover rows of shelf space. You will be automatically led to them as you take that pathway, in whatever direction or subject you choose.

I have been fascinated—transfixed—by the lives of many men and women in the Civil War era. But my first and enduring fascination has been with Lincoln, without question the towering figure of the Civil War. It is said that more books have been written about him than perhaps any other figure in world history. In that seemingly endless sea of print about that great man, a handful stand out in my mind, books that I have avidly read in my quest to capture him in my mind. John Nicolay and John Hay, Lincoln's two personal secretaries, wrote a magisterial ten-volume biography that is also a sweeping account of the war—*Abraham Lincoln: A History*. William H. Herndon, Lincoln's law partner, tracked down dozens of people after the war who had known

Lincoln and from these collective memories wrote a three-volume biography, *Herndon's Life of Lincoln.* Every Lincoln biographer since has drawn heavily from the treasure trove of witnesses to Lincoln's life that Herndon collected and used as his sources.

Of the other later biographies written about Lincoln, half a dozen have been my guides: Albert J. Beveridge's *Abraham Lincoln, 1809-1858,* published in two volumes in 1928, is still the best, most comprehensive account of Lincoln's pre-presidential years. Sandburg's sweeping six-volume biography repells many historians because it appears to take such liberties with historical truth as claiming to know what Lincoln was thinking. That is indeed a risky business, but I sometimes think Sandburg really did know. James G. Randall's four-volume *Lincoln the President* is an authoratative masterpiece of Lincoln scholarship.

Lincoln's life also comes in shorter doses.The three best single-volume biographies, in my mind, are *Abraham Lincoln,* by Benjamin Thomas, published in 1952; *With Malice Toward None: The Life of Abraham Lincoln,* by Stephen Oates, published in 1977; and David Donald's *Lincoln,* published in 1995, the most recent and probably now the standard one-volume work, by perhaps the greatest of the Lincoln scholars.

If I was to pick a Confederate figure who would loom as large in the Southern mind as Lincoln did in the Union and now does in the national memory, it would be Robert E. Lee. Fortunately, he has not been neglected by writers and historians, beginning with what is still the most exhaustive, readable, and rewarding, if utterly adoring, study of his life—Douglas Southall Freeman's four-volume *R.E. Lee .*

But the fascinating figures of the Civil War are legion. Name one—any one—and there is a book to satisfy your deepest curiosity. Reading biographies is an excellent way to capture a time in history. A few in the panoply of great Civil War figures have told their own stories. Two of the best autobiographical works to come from the war in my mind were written by two preeminent Union commanders, Ulysses S. Grant (*Personal Memoirs of U.S. Grant*) and William Tecumseh Sherman (*Memoirs of General W.T. Sherman*). They are rightly viewed today as classics of military biography.

The cache of memoirs and letters by the players and actors in the Civil War is a rich and rewarding treasure. Personally I am partial to the memoirs and letters of women in the war, they who stayed behind and perhaps suffered most of all. Two primary works by women, one a Southerner, one a Northerner, stand out most vividly in my mind. Mary Chesnut, a gifted South Carolinian, kept a journal, an absolutely classic record of the war and its anguish as seen and experienced by a genteel Southern woman. It is available as *Mary Chesnut's Civil War*, edited by C. Vann Woodward. Her Northern counterpart, to my way of thinking, is Elizabeth Blair Lee, of the formidable and influential Blair family of Washington. She wrote daily letters to her naval officer husband, Samuel Phillips Lee, that, like Mary Chesnut's journal, stand as a rich and classic account of what a prominent Northern woman was seeing, experiencing, and feeling. Her letters have been collected and edited into a single volume by Virginia Jeans Laas under the title *Wartime Washington: The Civil War Letters of Elizabeth Blair Lee*. And speaking of wartime Washington, a delightful look at the nation's capital during the Civil War is Margaret Leech's *Reveille in Washington, 1860-1865*, a classic secondary work published in 1941. Also read it to catch the flavor of the times.

This modest, highly truncated listing of books can only be suggestive. There are oceans of material on the war on which to cast your own bark. These are only a few of my particular lighthouses on the shore, some of the more salient landmarks of my own personal study. Yours can be as different and unique, and your study as rewarding, as you wish to make it. The raw material is all there, burgeoning and beckoning.